APOCALYPSE DELAYED

APOCALYPSE DELAYED

WHY THE LEFT IS STILL IN TROUBLE

NICK TYRONE

Biteback Publishing

First published in Great Britain in 2017 by
Biteback Publishing Ltd
Westminster Tower
3 Albert Embankment
London SE1 7SP
Copyright © Nick Tyrone 2017

ISBN 978-1-78590-291-8

10 9 8 7 6 5 4 3 2 1

A CIP catalogue record for this book is available from the British Library.

Set in Minion Pro

Printed and bound in Great Britain by

CPI Group (UK) Ltd, Croydon CR0 4YY

MIX
Paper from
responsible sources
FSC
www.fsc.org
FSC® C020471

CONTENTS

PART I

UNPACKING THE 2017 GENERAL ELECTION

CHAPTER 1

WELL, THAT DIDN'T GO AS PLANNED

I was one of the many who thought that Theresa May was going to end up with a large majority after the 2017 general election, right up until the very end. My feeling at the time was that even though she had fought a terrible campaign, the unelectability of Corbyn combined with the Brexit issue would see her home regardless. Needless to say, that was not the case. I suppose I had never seen Theresa May as anything special at all, and was always confused by her massive approval ratings, and so I completely failed to understand the shift in public mood away from her in the late stages of the election campaign as a result. My analogy around this is that Theresa May's appeal was like Westlife's music: I couldn't hear what was good about it, and yet millions of people seemed to love it, so I priced that into the deal. When a new Westlife album was about to be reviewed by a bunch of Westlife fans, I just figured they'd love it, even if I thought it was rubbish. Turns out they thought it was crap as well, go figure.

The key event during the campaign for May was the launch of the Conservative manifesto. Up until that point she was ahead in the polls by a large margin and the campaign strategy of keeping her to stale mantras and very stage-managed events and media appearances seemed to be working. The problem with the manifesto was that it contained some very radical policies, particularly one regarding social care that came very quickly to be dubbed the 'dementia tax'; a call for older people who require social care to repay the state for the assistance out of the proceeds of their estate post-mortem. It is difficult to imagine a policy more perfectly designed to irritate the Tory core vote, and after that, the right-of-centre press began to question her much more vigorously, something she wasn't in any way prepared for, and which furthermore the entire campaign strategy was specifically designed to avoid. She had tried to glide past the electorate with as little scrutiny as possible while simultaneously pitching some very bold ideas that could not possibly go unscrutinised, even by a media that was treating the whole election as a done deal.

The exit poll, arriving on our screens at 10 p.m. on

election day, was a shock to absolutely everyone. Tory campaigners had been feeling bullish throughout the day, while most Labour people on the ground had sheepishly admitted that things looked bleak from their end. No one really saw the hung parliament coming, but there it was: the Tories were projected to be about ten to fifteen seats short of a majority. Labour was apparently to gain seats not lose them, despite the constituencies in question having had no money poured into them. It looked as if the Lib Dems had avoided the electoral meltdown many had predicted. In addition, the SNP were said to have done notably worse than almost any pundit had thought possible.

By the time the morning of 9 June rolled around, it was clear that the exit poll was very close to being spot on. In the wake of Corbyn doing wildly better than anyone had expected – including almost certainly Jeremy Corbyn himself – several things immediately occurred. One was for many on the left to throw around the word 'hope' with abandon – as if equalling the 2010 seat haul, losing the third general election on the trot and furthermore welcoming in a Tory–DUP minority administration was a wonderful thing to have happened from their perspective. Another was for most people within the Labour Party to instantly cave into all resistance to Jeremy Corbyn, as if the only problem they had ever had with his leadership was his supposed lack of ability to win an election and nothing else (and despite the fact that he hadn't even managed to win an election, or even come relatively close to doing so). Some members of the Parliamentary Labour Party (PLP) were brave enough to point out that Corbyn hadn't actually won and indeed, had done no better than Gordon Brown in terms of seats – Chris Leslie and Mike Gapes, most notably – but most began bowing to the now unquestionable authority of Jeremy Corbyn straight off. For those Labour MPs like Leslie who had stuck their neck out and refused to toe the line, there were immediate consequences.

Alongside all of this came wild declarations from various quarters that Brexit was now 'over', sidestepping the unfortunate fact that the two parties that will effectively be governing the country for the next who knows how long had both campaigned in the election on an explicitly pro-Brexit ticket, as had the Labour Party, that latter fact conveniently forgotten for the moment by the anti-Brexit left. For those of us who had hoped that the 2017 general election might bring about some sort of re-shaping of the Labour Party into a more centrist outfit, or failing that a realignment of British politics involving a split in one or both of the two major parties, we are left adjusting to a result that entrenched the left/right two-party system more than ever and has set up the next general election, whenever it should occur, to be based on one simple question: do you want Jeremy Corbyn to be Prime Minister or not? I had hoped that, at the very, very least, this question would have been answered by the 2017 general election definitively.

The current situation places centrists in a very difficult position. Supporting Jeremy Corbyn isn't excusable on any level, but supporting a Tory–DUP combination isn't a great option either. The Lib Dems seem incapable of rising to the challenge of becoming a voice for those of us in neither of the major camps, deciding instead to remain a third-best soft-left choice. The hoped-for new centrist party that had been discussed in certain corridors now looks further away than ever, just at a time when it is needed most.

So, what should centrists do now? In this book, I'll set out the options and try to decide which seem the most plausible. Despite the sudden polarisation of British politics, I feel I am speaking for a lot of people out there who would like to see public services improve, but without a dramatic rise in taxation that would be self-defeating to that very same cause as it would cause more high earners to move abroad or engage in tax avoidance on a greater scale; who want to see young people get a better start to their adult lives, yet would rather that didn't come in the form of free tuition fees, which is essentially a bung to the upper middle classes; who would like to see Brexit, if it needs to happen, occur in a way that is not destructive to the economy of the United Kingdom.

Perhaps the oddest thing about the 2017 general election is that it could end up doing very long-term damage to the left and its agenda. In a sense, the result showed just how much of what the left wants in policy terms is now very, very popular; it is clear there is a real hunger for an end to austerity, and with it a strong desire for a Labour government that will spend Treasury pounds improving public services, debt and deficit worries aside. The problem with this, beyond the obvious, basic economics-related one, is that the left have looked at the result not as a vindication of their agenda but rather as an endorsement for a single individual. A fundamental thesis of this book is that Jeremy Corbyn remains Jeremy Corbyn, Labour surge be damned, and that he is still a net drag on the electoral fortunes of the Labour Party as opposed to the primary reason for their unexpected, out-of-the-blue 40 per cent national vote share in the 2017 general election. Thus, the fact that the left's big moment may have arrived and yet they have misinterpreted an appetite for left-wing policies as a hunger for a Corbyn premiership is, as I will argue throughout this book, a rather tragic thing.

The left, seemingly in the ascendance at present, is

still in trouble. The election may have seemed like a pretty definitive push back for the Conservative Party to some, but there were some objective victories for them in amongst the rubble. One, they are still in charge of the country – a not so insignificant thing in and of itself. Two, the collapse of UKIP has eliminated any serious rival on the right, uniting the right for the first time since the 2010 general election. It is worth bearing in mind that remaining in government as the largest party and destroying UKIP would have been considered a great result for the Tories going into the 2015 general election. Perspective is everything in politics, now more than ever.

CHAPTER 2

THE EXTREME FOLLY OF THE 'PROGRESSIVE ALLIANCE' LAID BARE

After the exit poll came out at 10 p.m. on 8 June 2017, the BBC interviewed several pundits on what it all meant. Zoe Williams of *The Guardian* was the first that night to bring up the idea of the 'progressive alliance', saying that a supposed informal pact between the 'progressive' parties – Labour, Lib Dem, SNP, Green, Plaid Cymru – had led directly to the Tories failing to get a majority. It was a concept that had done the rounds of the left-wing press throughout the entire campaign, as if it was a real, organised thing, when this is highly questionable.

The progressive alliance was a loose (very loose) pact that supposedly existed between the main 'progressive' parties at the 2017 general election. Who those parties were depended on where you fitted within the left (and how much you disliked the Lib Dems and/or the Scottish Nationalists), but it definitely contains at the very least Labour and the Greens. Within a first past the post voting system, it is very difficult for smaller parties to win seats, and often a vote for them can be seen to have 'taken' a vote from another progressive party, one that could have been victorious in said seat, leading to an 'unprogressive' result (code for: the Tories win instead). An example of the progressive alliance in action was the Lib Dems not running a candidate in Brighton Pavilion in order to give Caroline Lucas a clear run.

Another two examples of the progressive alliance in action were Labour activists working hard to remove Nick Clegg in Sheffield Hallam and Lib Dem MP Greg Mulholland in Leeds North West, in both cases successfully. The SNP and Labour also fought each other viciously across Scotland, Labour getting a better result this time from a repeat of the 2015 battle they had fought against the Nats. The Labour vote went up massively in the south-west of England in the 2017 contest; one of the first things you would definitely have done if you were trying to get a majority going for a progressive alliance would have been to have Labour step aside completely in that part of the country in order to give the Lib Dems, who have the data, members and activists there to actually win seats, a free run. All of this goes directly against the entire grain of the 'progressive alliance' narrative. Unless the Lib Dems, having gone into government with the Conservatives from 2010 until 2015, aren't part of this fabled alliance, of course (a perfectly plausible claim), in which case the faux concordat in question looks to have come nowhere remotely close to winning power. On the morning of 9 June, Emily Thornberry said to media outlets that if the smaller parties wanted to back a Labour Queen's Speech then they were welcome to – but there would be no discussions, no deal. A greater rebuke to the concept of a progressive alliance you will not find than that.

The real problem with the whole concept of a progressive alliance comes down to this: if there is so little difference between the parties involved in this loose alliance, why not all unite into one party and be done with it? It is much, much easier to prevent a Tory majority by consolidating the progressive vote under one banner, particularly in a first past the post voting system. The obvious answer is that not all of these parties actually are the same – not even close – and that the concept of a 'progressive majority' is a false one not just in terms of its actuality on the ground but even as a theoretical concept. This isn't just because of the supposed small-'c' conservatism of the British electorate, either: it is not clear what defines this progressivism that supposedly holds sway with all of these voters. Is it about Brexit? Labour advocated a hard Brexit in its manifesto, stating that Britain would leave the single market and freedom of movement would end if they formed a government, so that seems a stretch. Was it just about wanting to end austerity? This is much closer to being a uniting factor between all of the parties in question; however, this isn't as simple as just advocating more public spending, and all of the 'progressive' entities had very different ideas on this matter. This is particularly true given a few of them are strictly regional parties, and thus were often arguing for funding for projects that would drain money away from the centre, places where Labour might want to commit spending. The Liberal Democrats were one of the architects of the current austerity era we still live in, having been part of the Lib–Con government which started it – again, you're left with the problem of whether to keep the Lib Dems in or leave them out of this virtuous circle. Was it just that all of them weren't either the Tories or UKIP? Sadly, this is the factor probably closest to being the real element of supposed consensus. So again, why not all just vote Labour as a way of preventing a Tory government then, rather than messing about with an informal pact that wasn't even really an informal pact?

The main narrative of the 2017 general election, beyond Theresa May's innate woodenness and the gamble that backfired spectacularly, was the better than expected Labour result, with that party ending up with 40 per cent of the national vote. That number does not speak of some sort of alliance between parties; in fact, it shows that most left-leaning people throughout the country voted for the Labour Party. The best way to demonstrate this is to remove Labour from the picture and see what's left of your so-called progressive alliance: the Lib Dems took five seats off the Tories, while the SNP lost thirteen to Ruth Davidson's party. No one else took any seats from the Conservatives apart from Labour. By my count, that means the progressive alliance sans Corbyn's army lost a net of eight seats to the Tories. That, if I may be so bold, is a fairly poor showing.

Corbyn was right to shut down any talk of a progressive alliance between parties from the very outset of the election campaign. It never works, and it didn't work again in 2017. Besides the fact that Labour have now within their means the ability to hoover up every left-leaning vote in the country as there aren't many left out there to gather and Corbynmania is presumably still riding high, taking their revenge on the Scottish Nationalists along the way, they have shown time and time again that they cannot work with other parties at

Westminster. The inability to get the Lib Dems to seriously consider a coalition with them in 2010 is a case in point; the total incapability of the shadow Cabinet to even pretend to reach out to other non-Tory parties after the hung parliament in 2017 is another. Labour will try to wipe out the rest of the 'progressive alliance' as much as it can and furthermore, they would be foolish not to do so.

One final thing to say of note on the progressive alliance: Labour weren't even allied within their own ranks, never mind being able to strike invisible deals with their supposed sister parties. It is worth noting in the wake of Labour's election 'victory' – or more aptly, 'brilliant defeat' – that many Labour MPs ran explicitly on the premise that voters could plump for them without there being any danger of Jeremy Corbyn becoming Prime Minister. Something tells me that one won't work next time round.

CHAPTER 3

HOW CORBYN BECAME
THE KING OF LABOUR

Very few Labour MPs in the immediate shadow of Corbyn's better than expected election result were brave enough to still be critical of the Labour leader in public. Mike Gapes and Chris Leslie were the most courageous, with Leslie taking to the *Today* programme to say:

> We shouldn't pretend that this is a famous victory. It is good as far as it's gone but it's not going to be good enough. Five years of Conservative government, I just can't, I'm afraid, be a cheerleader for that particular outcome because this was an open goal for all of us. We should have been getting in there.*

---

* BBC *Today* programme, 12 June 2017

The very same day Leslie made these comments to the media, the branch of Momentum in his seat, Nottingham East, sent this charming note around, both to Leslie and to its membership:

Open letter to Chris Leslie MP
Please note that only your name and branch will be public.

Dear Chris,

As you must have been, we were delighted to see such a resounding victory for the Labour Party in Nottingham East, with our party securing 71% of the vote and an 8% swing from the Tories.

We are writing this letter to you because, after the generous and gracious statements by many of the PLP who had previously expressed misgivings about Jeremy's leadership, we were saddened to hear your comments on the Today *programme.*

It is difficult to imagine what positive outcomes you thought that interview might achieve. Whilst many of us might disagree, we would have no objections to you expressing these views in a Labour Party meeting, but ask that you do not do so in the media.

We are disappointed that you felt you couldn't affirm that Jeremy 'is a credible Prime Minister' and chose instead to emphasise your 'disagreements on security [and the] economy'.

The Labour Party has always been a broad church, and long may that continue.

We ask that you refrain from expressing such disunity in the media. The place for a frank discussion of such matters is inside party meetings.

Hilary Benn in his victory speech asked us to 'build on what we have achieved this night to maintain the unity as a party that we have shown in this campaign, and never to cease in our yearning for a fair society'.

We, as Nottingham East members, ask that you work with us to consolidate the united campaigning force that we have built in this election campaign. Your constituents desperately need you to help build that unity to prepare for the next election and a Labour victory.

Yours sincerely,
Councillor Adele Williams and Sherwood Branch Secretary
Chantal Lee, PPC for Newark and St Ann's Branch Secretary
Tom Unterrainer, Berridge Branch, Editor Corbyn's Campaign
Councillor Graham Chapman
Rosemary Chapman

The message here was clear: insult the dear leader again and deselection will be headed your way. Only blind loyalty to Jeremy will be tolerated from here on out.

Clive Lewis, newly re-elected Labour MP for Norwich

South, responded by saying on 5 Live later that same day: 'I think Chris Leslie is a sad, lonely, bitter man.'* Remember, Leslie hadn't even gone as far as to openly question Corbyn's leadership – he simply pointed out that being sixty-odd seats short of a majority doesn't in fact count as a victory. As Lewis himself had resigned from the shadow Cabinet only four months previous, his comments were not only highly hypocritical, they also showed what was in store for Labour MPs who show any signs of not sticking to the script that Corbyn 'won' the 2017 general election from here on in.

Since September 2015, most members of the PLP have played a game with the leadership question: loyal to the Labour Party, but desperately wanting to change the leader. The hope was that losing an election would cause a change at the top, and then Labour could elect someone more in line with most of their ideas around how the party should be run (although what this would be was never really made clear. 'Not Corbyn' was as far as it ever seems to have been developed). After the 'brilliant defeat', no one can sit on that fence any longer. This could be a real problem for Labour if the next general election does not take place within the next year or so – and the Tories do not need to put forward another

---

* Clive Lewis, Radio 5 Live, 12 June 2017

Queen's Speech until 2019 – particularly as Corbyn blew his one chance to unite the party in June 2017 in the immediate aftermath of the election: had he given people like Chuka Umunna and Yvette Cooper shadow Cabinet roles (which they would likely have taken up) he would have genuinely been able to bring the party together. Not doing so demonstrated that unity of the Labour Party is of no interest to Corbyn and his inner circle. Their mission remains as it ever was: total domination of the party by the hard left for the rest of time. They have simply been nimbler about achieving this than anyone could have guessed they would be, running on a Miliband-esque manifesto that exploited the weaknesses in the Conservative manifesto, and gambling on a very, very, very fuzzy Brexit position paying off (as indeed it did, with Leavers in northern and Midlands seats buying the hard Brexit guff while at the same time Labour became the 'stop Brexit' vote where that was helpful to them). In other words, Corbyn proved he was a decent campaigner. Yet as soon as the election was over and the dust settled, Corbyn immediately demonstrated his weaknesses again, including the inability to work with anyone who is not of his ilk, and his total disinterest in the workings of the House of Commons, making it fairly easy for the Tories to form a minority government with little fear of tangible opposition despite the razor-thin majority held by their cobbled-together 'coalition'. Corbyn further demonstrated his remarkable inability to be anything other than a truly awful leader of the opposition generally, having what could almost be described as a genuine talent for letting the government off the hook in any given situation.

By shunning the Yvettes and the Chukas when he had the chance to bring them on side, Corbyn has created several problems for himself. One is that those big beasts of the PLP are still free agents and have no personal stake in a future Labour government of which they know they will not be a part. This could well be material on issues like Brexit, where the Tories will wish to divide and conquer with the PLP; uniting all elements of the party inside of the shadow Cabinet would have made it easier for Corbyn to whip whatever stance he wanted to take on the Tories' manoeuvres in this regard. As things stand, he has left himself very open to rebellion, or at the very least disarray, particularly if the mood inside the PLP sours towards Corbyn as a second snap election recedes from view.

CHAPTER 4

THE 2017 GENERAL ELECTION, BLOW BY PAINFUL BLOW

After the 2017 general election was sprung upon every-one by Theresa May, the immediate polls looked absolutely terrible for Labour. They had been poor for the party around that period anyhow, but once the election was called, something interesting kicked in right away: the very plausible spectre of the entire UKIP vote going directly to the Conservatives. A YouGov poll taken a few days before Theresa May's announcement had UKIP on 10 per cent nationally;[*] another taken by the same poll-ing company a little over a week later had them down to 5 per cent.[†] Although the UKIP polling figures went up

---

[*]   YouGov poll, 12–13 April 2017
[†]   YouGov poll, 20–24 April 2017

and down from there, as did all of the parties' numbers throughout the campaign, there was an unquestionable downwards trajectory, noted by everyone in the universe apart from Paul Nuttall. The hollowing out of the UKIP vote nationwide was interpreted correctly by the pollsters, with the anti-EU party ending up with less than 2 per cent of the national vote on polling day.

At the same time, while the Labour poll numbers had been stagnating in the mid-twenties for several months leading up to the election being called anyhow, the announcement of the plebiscite seemed to solidify them at around 25 per cent or so nationally. Worse was some of the regional polling: a YouGov poll of specific English regions mid-campaign saw the Tories up fifteen points on 2015 figures in the north-east of England, coming within a mere two points of Labour* in the area. Bearing in mind that this has traditionally been one of Labour's core vote regions, it now looked like the predicted landslide victory for May's Conservatives was going to be a cakewalk, as even the expected bounce that calling the election was supposed to have given to the Lib Dems failed to materialise in the polls.

Once the campaigns got truly underway, the advantage the Tories held over all of their rivals appeared to be

---

* YouGov poll, published 15 May 2017

constantly cemented. Labour's early attempts to reach out to the electorate were plagued by a seemingly unending series of gaffes by senior members of the shadow Cabinet, most notably a radio interview with Diane Abbott in which she mistakenly spoke about paying a new crop of police officers £30 a year, and an unfortunate exchange involving Emily Thornberry where she laughed out loud at the idea of celebrating St George's Day. Meanwhile, Theresa May was shuttled around from stage-managed event to stage-managed event, mostly muttering 'strong and stable' and 'coalition of chaos' over and over again to a press gang that was willing, seemingly, to just accept it. A fortunately timed run-in with Jean-Claude Juncker at No. 10 was even more helpful, May able to use it to big up the 'we won't be bossed around by Brussels' narrative. May appeared on *The One Show* on the BBC with her husband in tow; they spoke in banal tones about their wardrobes – and people ate it up. It felt for a few weeks as if Lynton Crosby was controlling the universe. On 4 May, the local elections came and went, and this seemed to crystallise the Conservatives' greatest hopes and Labour's biggest fears: the Tories gained over 500 seats, while Labour lost over 300. Added to that, UKIP lost every seat they were defending, the SNP did poorly and the Lib Dems lost seats in an election in which they were expected at the very least to gain a few. The Tories definitively won the May local elections at the expense of every single rival.

Then came the launch of the party manifestos and, with it, a wholly unexpected wobble by the governing party. The Tory manifesto included: a commitment to bring back fox hunting, which only served to remind a lot of ex-Labour voters why they didn't tend to vote Conservative in the first place; the aforementioned 'dementia tax'; the triple-lock promise from the Cameron era – a pledge to ensure pensions rise each year with the rate of inflation, or average earnings increase, or 2.5 per cent, whichever is highest of the three – being broken (while Labour committed to it, notably). A very poorly executed media appearance by the Prime Minister on Channel 4 in which she and Corbyn took questions from the audience followed by a grilling from Jeremy Paxman occurred in the midst of all this, a period which saw Labour suddenly polling much better than they had done at any time since 2014. In desperation, the Tories dug up everything they could muster from Jeremy Corbyn's past: the IRA stuff, in particular. This referred to Jeremy Corbyn and John McDonnell's past support for the IRA during the period when the Troubles were active, the Conservatives trying to counter the claim made by the Labour duo that they had been agents for peace in Ireland. None of it seemed to make the Labour polling numbers drop back to pre-election levels. In fact, they seemed to actually make them improve further, as people increasingly felt they were being patronised by the Tory campaign.

Figures for the predicted Conservative majority were revised downwards by almost everyone in Westminster; in some quarters, there was even talk – deemed hysterical at the time – of the possibility of a hung parliament. Even more bizarre thinking was done on the left around a possible freak Corbyn victory. Many a pundit who writes for *The Guardian* penned an article during this period along the lines of 'The latest unexpected victory after Brexit and Trump will be one for the left this time round.' (These were usually authored by journalists who had been disparaging about Corbyn previously.) All of a sudden, the election that had seemed a foregone conclusion appeared to be on a knife's edge. Some speculated – I was amongst them – that all of this was ultimately going to be to the Conservatives' advantage come polling day; wasn't one of their big worries at the start having the result assumed to be a foregone conclusion, thus instilling complacency amongst Tory voters, leading them to stay home on polling day? Surely now that Corbyn really did look like he could plausibly win, or at the very least deny the Conservative Party a victory, the Tory vote would be out in droves.

To add to the confusion, the polls were telling us wildly divergent things as June dawned: ICM had the Tories with a double-figure lead while Survation had Labour within a point of the Conservatives (although even the most optimistic polls for Labour never had them ahead, not once in the whole campaign). Despite all this, the consensus in Westminster was that Labour couldn't possibly do as well as some of the polls were now predicting; that, again, the British people's innate conservatism would set in on the day, and with it a Tory majority of between thirty and 100 would emerge.

And then, *that* exit poll. I will admit, the first thing I did when it popped up on my TV screen was laugh heartily. May had run an arrogant and shoddy campaign that on one hand was an attempt to glide past the elec-torate as untested as possible, and yet on the other she had hubristically thought she could still propose any-thing she liked and no one would care.

Then reality set in for me, quickly. Oddly, the party that was going to come out the best from the wreckage of all this, in the long term at least, was very probably the Tories, simply because you could see that they would almost certainly learn all the right lessons from the set-back they were then in the process of experiencing. Next time, they just might get someone with some charis-ma to be leader, someone who can campaign at a level necessary to win a general election. Don't assume that just because the leader of the opposition is rubbish, an election will be a breeze; the public hates complacency in a ruling party.

Meanwhile, Labour and the Lib Dems will almost certainly learn all of the wrong lessons from the 2017 general election. Within the PLP, we have already seen a massive overcorrection for the way Corbyn is viewed: he's gone from being a hopeless stooge who needs to be moved aside if victory is to be achieved again to an untouchable campaigning genius who just needs 'one more heave' in order to become the next Labour Prime Minister. Objectively speaking, the 2017 general election campaign showed us that Corbyn is merely a mediocre Labour leader as opposed to a disastrous one; more like a Neil Kinnock than a Michael Foot. Only, the comparison with Kinnock is unfair to Kinnock in one very important respect: at least Kinnock rebuilt the Labour Party, laying the foundations for eventual Labour victory, by rooting out the party's most pressing problems over the course of his leadership. Corbyn, on the other hand, will continue to revisit all of his worst mistakes on the presumption that the 2017 general election campaign was nothing but a rip-roaring success, despite the end result being the continuation of a Tory-led government. There is no rebuilding going on under Corbyn, only further dismantling, all justified by the thirty-odd seats gained in June 2017. For Labour, we could be in for a situation I would term as 'apocalypse delayed': the meltdown expected in 2017 simply being put off until the next general election comes along.

As for the Liberal Democrats, the 2017 election campaign has been chalked up as a relative success, despite Farron having a very poor campaign throughout. Their small net gains were down to two main factors: good campaigning/use of resource and activists, and the SNP slump. Without either, wipe-out could have occurred. At the very least, the 2017 election allowed the Lib Dems to get a new leader and a chance at a fresh start – more than can be said for Labour.

CHAPTER 5

WHAT HAPPENS TO BREXIT NOW?

Europe is the issue that had split the right in Britain for years and years, whereas the left had united behind pro-Europeanism after the Social Chapter had been introduced in the late 1980s (excepting a small hard-left faction that remained Eurosceptic, led by people like Jeremy Corbyn). The rise of UKIP from the start of the Lib–Con coalition until the EU referendum was the direct result of this split. While the grassroots of the right became increasingly Eurosceptic, the leadership of the Conservative Party tended to state that Britain needed to remain in the European Union for practical reasons (although this view was always put forward weakly, David Cameron being the all-time case study for this sort of behaviour). There was, however, a period before the 2017 general election when it looked very possible that the left would end up becoming hurt by a fight that was started within the right more badly than the right itself. While the Leave result in the EU referendum has led to the implosion of UKIP, and the right mostly uniting behind the Conservative Party once again, by early 2017 the left had splintered as a result of the referendum result. Labour realised that it needed to keep its Leave-voting contingent in the north, the Midlands and Wales on side by promising a hard Brexit, but meanwhile its young, urban voters wanted Labour to promise to reverse Brexit altogether. It was predicted that Labour could end up being perfectly electorally pinched as a result, with the Tories getting the Leave voters and the Lib Dems getting the Remain ones (it was described by some pundits as the '0 per cent strategy').

Surprisingly to many, myself included, precisely the opposite occurred: Labour's fudge on Brexit worked as perfectly as could be imagined. Working-class Leave voters bought into the party's weakly trumpeted pro-Brexit shtick, while Remain voters coalesced around Labour almost completely. In what is being now touted as the election about Brexit that wasn't, it is amazing how much Labour benefited from the Brexit issue in the end.

What makes all this even more amazing is just how ineptly the European subject was approached by Labour in that early 2017 pre-election campaign period.

Corbyn said he would three-line whip his MPs to vote for May's brief Article 50 Bill in January; we all knew that was coming, as soon as the referendum result was announced. He was the one who had called for Article 50 to be triggered the day after the plebiscite, after all, thus paving the way for such a manoeuvre. Having said all that, I was still taken aback by how easily he rolled over on certain aspects of the Article 50 Bill's passage through the Commons. The government allowed just five days for all of the debates. This was a major Bill that will almost certainly be instrumental in deciding the near future of the country, remember, and Labour was the official opposition. Yet, in a rush to appear to be as pro-Brexit as possible, they didn't even try to block the government from tabling a timetable on the matter that was faintly ludicrous. What should have made it worse was that Corbyn, Emily Thornberry and others were all over the media at the time, talking up the opposition they were going to provide against the Bill, Thornberry going so far as to describe it in one interview as 'hand-to-hand combat'.* This all felt farcical when compared to their actions inside the House of Commons.

Even when New Labour achieved power from 1997 until 2010, the left's relationship with the EU was

---

* Emily Thornberry, *Newsnight* interview, 24 January 2017

riddled with difficulties. Although Blair was vocally pro-European, he still couldn't resist occasionally using it as a dumping ground for any political problems he faced, and as a result he never really articulated why being in the EU was a good thing for Britain. It didn't help, of course, that Gordon Brown was much more Eurosceptic and thus there was, even at the height of Labour's pro-Europeanism, a pull away from getting Britain more heavily involved in the running of the EU. Britain would push the bits it wanted, such as eastern expansion of the union; it would leave the stuff it was less interested in, i.e. most of it, to France and Germany.

Had there been a leader of the Labour Party in place who was a passionate pro-European when the EU referendum rolled around, things might have been different in many ways. It is noteworthy in the wake of the 2017 general election campaign, for instance, to see what Corbyn is like as a campaigner when he really cares about the result, and to come to some obvious conclusions.

When it became clear that the 2017 general election would result in a hung parliament, for a few hours the left rejoiced about the supposed 'end of Brexit', or at the very least the end of hard Brexit, and some seemed to believe that the result meant Britain would assuredly stay in the single market if nothing else. The quick formation of the basis for the Tory–DUP government before lunchtime the following day put a damper on this feeling, at least amongst the more politically literate on the left. It became clear pretty quickly that the right had the numbers to continue with Brexit, even if the question about single market membership did seem up in the air suddenly, if only for practical reasons, as Theresa May probably lacks the numbers in the Commons to get her hard Brexit now.

But how important is Brexit for Labour anyhow? Won't it fade in importance after 2019? Probably not, for several reasons. One, a transitional deal is likely to be in place for a long time, keeping the subject alive for longer than many had expected. Two, the sudden question of how involved key figures from Labour will now be in the negotiations themselves is important. The Tories have extended an olive branch to the PLP in this regard, trying to get Labour figures more and more involved in the Brexit negotiations for two reasons: one, so that Labour owns the result of it all in some ways, particularly if it involves retaining freedom of movement and jurisdiction of the ECJ for any period of time; and two, to create rifts in the party, attacking Labour unity. Had Corbyn invited moderates into the shadow Cabinet, as suggested earlier, this danger would have been greatly minimised; as it is, it remains a big risk to Labour's fragile unity.

As for what actually happens with Brexit itself, everyone in Westminster is currently speculating about whether the election result means that a softer Brexit is now inevitable, contrary to May's rhetoric earlier this year. One thing to bear in mind on this point: the EU Commission now has one massive trump card to play as a result of the election result. The stability of the current government relies entirely on the DUP staying on board. While this is very likely to last longer than many think, due to the DUP finding Corbyn's past dealings with the IRA distasteful to say the least, they do have one solid red line: no hard border between Northern and Southern Ireland. This means that 'no deal' is effectively off the table: if the UK cannot agree to at least a transitional deal before March 2019, then a hard border would be enforced by the EU in early 2019 (or earlier, if it looks as though no transitional deal is forthcoming). Should this scenario transpire, the DUP would have to bring the government down (as a result of regional pressure on the issue), and then the Tories would be forced to confront an election at the worst possible time (and with Theresa May very possibly still as leader as well, if they haven't managed to depose her by then). The idea that all of this will not play a factor in the negotiations is to be wilfully naïve, particularly given the state of the British government.

Corbyn is a lifelong Eurosceptic whose main electoral selling point is his supposed honesty. And yet, he managed to get a much better than expected election result by completely fudging the defining issue of our time. Since the election, Labour have continued to try to look both ways on Brexit, but this is unlikely to be something they can do for ever. As the negotiations with the European Commission proceed, two things are almost certain to happen: one, the choices about what to do in regards to Brexit will become tangible, and Labour will be forced off the fence on things like single market membership; two, the public's understanding on these matters is going to grow enormously over the next two years, so Labour will not be able to continue bullshitting on this quite so effectively as they are now. Once more people understand that tariff-free access will only come by accepting free movement of workers, Labour will be required to say something coherent on the matter. At that point, they will no longer be able to be all things to both Leavers and Remainers.

CHAPTER 6

PRESIDENTIAL POLITICS

One of the key features of the 2017 general election was what could be termed the 'presidential aspect': the relevant party leaders playing a greater role symbolically in both of the main parties' campaigns ('Theresa May's Team' as opposed to the Conservatives) and, subsequently, the vote for either party being seen as a vote for 'Jeremy' or 'Mrs May' (or explicitly *not* for them, as the case may be).

The Tories were keen early on to emphasise Theresa May's then popularity and Corbyn's supposed lack thereof (not to mention the non-popularity of most of the other party leaders besides Corbyn as well). This ended up severely hurting their campaign in the final two weeks, when it emerged that basing your campaign around personality when your candidate sorely lacks that feature is a bad idea. Lulled into a false sense of security by Corbyn's total inability to direct his party effectively, or for that matter even pretend to be a functional Leader of the Opposition, the Tories forgot that he is a good campaigner. Now that Corbyn is ensconced as Labour leader until at least the next general election, barring unforeseen circumstances, the Tories will have to figure out some way to counter Corbyn with a party leader with some charisma next time out, given the importance of this 'presidential' style of politics we seem stuck with.

I recall speaking to a Tory friend in late 2016 regarding who might emerge as a credible opposition party leader should the Corbyn revolution fall as flat as everyone at the time expected it to.

'A Ken Clarke-led Lib Dems would be an interesting prospect.'

I remember this throwaway line so vividly because the one Tory who was credible as a leader of a liberal faction capable of getting widespread support also happened to be seventy-six years of age at the time. Without wishing to be ageist in any way, the fact that Ken was the only person we could think of with the level of credibility needed to possibly pull such a thing off spoke to a dearth of talent in the House of Commons that does not get remarked upon enough.

One of the main reasons that Corbyn won the Labour leadership in 2015 is that he was up against three people who all, in their own ways, represented an extreme lack of inspiration and/or ideas. Worse, they all fell back on the time-honoured 'Well, the far left has all sorts of wonderful ideas but it's just not electable, is it?' routine, fatally misjudging the mood of the membership, not to mention unconsciously making a rod for their own backs once Corbyn did electorally better than expected. However, beyond the lack of ideas, it is worth judging for a moment how Yvette Cooper, Andy Burnham or Liz Kendall would have done in the 2017 general election had any of them become Labour leader in 2015. Of course, had any of them done so, we'd probably be in a very different place politically right now for all sorts of reasons, but let us put that to one side for the time being. This is a question whose answer will become one of those dividing lines in progressive politics over the next few years.

While the basic camps involved in this debate are usually on one hand the 'Corbyn was responsible for the gain of seats entirely' trope and on the other, '*Any* other leader but Corbyn would have actually *won* the election', I don't fall into either. I think Burnham, Cooper or Kendall would have lost the 2017 general election by roughly the same amount as Corbyn did; not much more and not much less. For while Corbyn is a bad leader that Labour would have to displace to genuinely move forward, the problems within the Labour Party run much deeper than that. I think a Cooper or a Kendall could have got more people in the centre to go Labour; swing voters who went with the Conservatives in 2017 yet might have been persuaded by a non-Corbyn Labour leader to vote red. On the other hand, they would have struggled to get the same youth turnout that Corbyn did. Like I say, I think it all would have come out about the same in the end, with Labour a significant number of seats short of victory and the Tories as the largest party.

It may be worthwhile here to digress briefly and talk about the qualities that make for a popular Prime Minister. In a poll taken by the BBC in 2002 to find out who the British public thought were the greatest ever Britons to date,[*] Winston Churchill was number one, with Cromwell in the top ten and the Duke of Wellington and Margaret Thatcher at fifteen and sixteen respectively. Picking from a very rich list of every Briton who has ever existed, the denizens of these isles chose to stock a quarter of their top sixteen picks with politicians, including giving the very highest spot to a former Prime Minister. I bring this up as a way of demonstrating that

---

[*]   BBC *100 Greatest Britons*, 2002

the British public doesn't hate politicians nearly as much as is widely assumed; they simply have a particular kind of politician they tend to like and a corresponding high disdain for those who get it wrong (as Theresa May found out for herself in the harshest way imaginable very recently).

The ideal Prime Minister has to be a strange and very rare mixture of extreme hubris and superhuman humility. An interesting thing about past popular Prime Ministers is just how much the public were willing to keep voting for them to retain power even when they did things the voters either didn't like or were at least highly suspicious of. A lot of Thatcher's programme falls into this category, yet she always seemed to have a plan and definable direction of travel, and so the public kept backing her, election after election, much to the chagrin of the left and all those who found her intolerable. You always knew what Thatcher was *about*, and that was the main thing.

Tony Blair had the same power; even after the wildly unpopular move of going to war with Saddam's Iraq had backfired significantly, he still managed to get a parliamentary majority in 2005 (worth noting here, the very last parliamentary majority Labour has yet to secure). On the other hand, Blair lacked the humility required, ultimately, which is the real reason his posterity lies in tatters. A British Prime Minister is meant to always have control but to be seen to be using that control for the good of the nation as a whole; Blair often seemed to be too personally motivated. One of the main reasons that Gordon Brown's reputation has been revitalised to such a degree since he left No. 10 is because he has been very humble and proper in what he's done since, taking on mostly unpaid roles in highly worthy organisations. I firmly believe that if Tony Blair had spent the past ten years volunteering for Greenpeace, he could just about manage the comeback he keeps threatening to make.

Theresa May is a particularly interesting study in the midst of all this. Before calling the election, she had approval ratings off the chart, becoming one of the most respected politicians for decades in Britain. She blew it during the campaign by proposing something off the wall and then U-turning on it. The strong and stable mantra died then, along with her shot at retaining her majority.

Every generation of politicians in Westminster since the 1980s at least seems to be diminished when compared to the one immediately before it, so that those who were mocked not so long ago appear like giants in retrospect. Part of this is the 'national treasure' phenomenon that happens to many ex-politicians in the UK, but there's more to it now than just that. I recall watching Gordon

Brown give a speech before the Scottish independence referendum in 2014 and thinking he seemed like a political God from another era; even David Cameron now looks like a barely imaginable political titan in the wake of the 2017 general election. Why is this happening?

Not enough people are willing to talk about this, but here it goes: being an MP is a really shitty job. The pay isn't great, at least for someone who would be considered managerial quality (in other words, anyone who is genuinely worthy of being an MP in the first place can make a great deal more in the private sector. And not have excrement shoved through their front door while they're at it). The hours are terrible, the travel back and forth from Westminster to one's constituency a real drag. You are under constant media scrutiny, with everything you say put under a microscope, and the consequences for screwing up being not just blowback for yourself and your family but for your party as well. And for all that, your power to change things is extremely minimal, at least if you're a backbencher (more so if you're an opposition backbencher). On top of all of that, being an MP screws with one's life in ways most of the public (and even a lot of Westminster insiders) won't be aware of. Try opening a business bank account if one of your directors is an MP and you'll understand what I mean. In the race to hold power to account, we've reduced MPs to a sort of sub-race of primate life, not even qualifying for basic things most British adults take for granted.

Walking down Broadway in Westminster one random day in the past year, I looked up from my phone to see one of Theresa May's most trusted No. 10 spads walking past me. As I watched him stroll past, it suddenly occurred to me that almost no one in the country would have recognised him, yet at the time he held infinitely more power than every Labour and Lib Dem MP combined (although, of course, he holds no power whatsoever these days, natch). All while making a lot more money and not having to conduct surgeries involving people's allotments. Why would anyone trade that in to be a Member of Parliament?

The executive branch of UK government feeds directly out of the Commons – thus, only people elected to the lower House can possibly be Prime Minister, and ergo, a weaker pool of MP talent will almost certainly lead in time to weaker people running the country. Or, at the very least, a weaker opposition, which over time has a similar effect. In other words, we need good people to be MPs so that good people can become Prime Ministers and Secretaries of State and Leaders of the Opposition.

What this all leads me to is a conclusion that some of you will find nauseating: the next Prime Minister to really capture the public mood successfully has every chance of being a celebrity of some description, i.e. someone who came to fame outside of politics and takes that notoriety along with them to obtain high public office. It's happened already in America, to deleterious effect: Trump would never have been elected President had he not already been a very famous person, a well-known 'dealmaker' at a time when such a thing became just what the nation wanted in a leader. You can easily see it happening in Britain; rather too easily, in fact. The individual's prior celebrity insulating them somewhat from the usual rigours of political scrutiny; the confidence that comes from having been in the public eye and been adored allowing said celebrity to come across as 'genuine' during media appearances; the 'known quantity' aspect shortcutting the need to build up trust with the public. Of course, as we've seen with Trump, most people who have been successful in another field who then enter politics often do so with the naïve notion that politics is really easy, coming in with the idea that if only a 'business-like' approach was taken, the country would be exponentially better off – only to find out that it's all mind-numbingly complex.

I have spent some time trying to find a thread through the 2015 general election result, the 2016 EU referendum result and the 2017 general election result. For many days after I started doing this exercise, I kept coming up blank. If the 2015 result was about maintaining stability, why vote to leave the EU in 2016 (a question David Cameron has no doubt asked himself a million times)? If the 2016 referendum result was really about a burning desire to leave the European Union, come what may, why vote for a result in 2017 that threw that into such doubt? But then it finally struck me: the only thing that unites all three results is presidential politics. In 2015, the media-savvy Cameron trumped the awkward Miliband; the Leave campaign had the stars, what with Farage and Boris up against a very bland Remain campaign; 2017 saw an animated and even occasionally funny Corbyn up against a dour and unappealing Theresa May. If this theory of mine holds any water, the left has a great deal to worry about. Imagine if the Tories can keep the DUP-based deal going for another few years. Then imagine that Ruth Davidson has managed to get a seat in Parliament via a by-election and from there manages to become Prime Minister. Picture Davidson up against Corbyn – he wouldn't look quite so attractive, particularly with a few more years of being an ineffectual Leader of the Opposition behind him. In other words, while the Conservative Party may have allowed someone who was a poor campaigner to become leader of the party once, that doesn't mean they are likely to make that same mistake again. The Tories have some, limited room to manoeuvre in presidential politics – the Labour Party no longer does. Perhaps no one emerges from the Tory fold good enough to make a difference. If I were working for the Labour Party, I would hardly take that for granted.

CHAPTER 7

WHERE THE LIBERAL DEMOCRATS FIT INTO ALL THIS

Back in the early days of May's premiership, some speculated that the then current woes of the Labour Party combined with a supposed shift to the right by the Tories would offer space for the Liberal Democrats to flourish. After Corbyn's Labour voted to trigger Article 50 with no amendments whatsoever, the Lib Dems were left as the only national party that had a fully anti-Brexit pedigree; this, it was thought, would allow the party to increase its share in the polls dramatically and for the parliamentary Lib Dem party to grow exponentially at the next general election, whenever that might occur.

After the snap election was called by Theresa May in April 2017, the most openly ecstatic party was the

Liberal Democrats. Forecasts were made of a doubling of seats – and that was by the pundits who were most pessimistic regarding the Lib Dems' election chances. Seat predictions of fifty or more were being hurtled about; unfortunately, none of those doing these sorts of projections seemed to have consulted a map of constituencies to find out where exactly all these Lib Dem gains were supposedly going to come from. Had they done so, they would have been more careful putting forth such pie-in-the-sky forecasts.

This is because, as we all now know, it didn't work out the way most people back in April predicted, with the party basically treading water, ending up with three more seats net than they had going into polling day. Nick Clegg symbolically lost his seat along the way. The Lib Dem surge did not emerge in the way most had predicted. Why?

The party went into the general election with three main problems: one, poor leadership; two, a lack of identity or policy platform beyond 'block Brexit'; three, a naïve optimism born of an innate lack of ambition.

Tim Farron's turn as leader of the Lib Dems didn't work out well for the party, yet the reason he was chosen by the membership in the summer of 2015 remains obvious: he is the very essence of Lib Deminess made human. After the coalition and the reduction to only eight MPs that followed it, the membership wanted to cling to things it found comfort in, and Tim Farron was the anthropomorphisation of that urge. This turned out to be a huge problem when, aside from Farron's basic problems as a party leader in general, the gap in the market that opened up for the Liberal Democrats turned out to be all wrong for Farron and his image. It was expected that after the 2015 general election result, Labour would move to the right. Thus, when Corbyn became leader, it was hard for Farron to adjust, given he had wanted to take back the soft-left territory the Lib Dems had owned pre-coalition. It is difficult to know whether this would ever have been possible (my guess is, no chance), but the ascension of Corbyn made it definitely impossible.

Yet the 2016 EU referendum result then offered the Lib Dems an unexpected lifeline, and they quickly jumped into the breach as *the* anti-Brexit party. On paper, this made perfect sense: the party had always been pro-European (although this was played down in the southwest), and with 48 per cent of the electorate theoretically up for grabs, this could have opened up a lot of territory for the Lib Dems to conquer. Unfortunately, this was a narrower reading of the situation than turned out to be sensible. For one, a lot of the people who voted to stay in the EU were young and on the left, and given that the Lib Dems had been in coalition with the Tories just over a year beforehand (not to mention tuition fee-related dislike), most of these people were never going to be converted into Lib Dem voters, regardless of what stances on Brexit were on offer across the table. Sadly, most Lib Dems seem desperate to regain votes from the left and, even sadder, truly believe that it is possible. Yet all of the Lib Dems' current seats are Tory-facing, even those in Scotland to some extent (in East Dunbartonshire, which Jo Swinson regained from the SNP at the 2017 election, Labour came fourth, behind the Tories).

Almost by default (as often happens in politics), the group of people that it became possible for the Lib Dems to realistically reach out to and pull to their side post-referendum were former Tory voters (or swing voters who might have voted Tory recently) who had been pro-Remain. The Lib Dems having been in the co-alition government would not have been a downside for these people but rather a plus, and with the right leader and set of policies, these people were probably reachable in reasonably large numbers. This was demonstrated in the Richmond Park by-election in December 2016 and, before that, in the Witney by-election in October 2016, in which the Lib Dems had come from nowhere into second on a huge swing from the Tories, in both cases clearly capturing the votes of this demographic. Another example of the rewards on offer from this strategy was watching Rachel Johnson, Boris's sister, convert to the Lib Dems simply off the back of the party's anti-Brexit position.

However, Tim Farron was always a bad fit for this direction and clearly never completely took to it. He is a politician of the soft left, a place too far away politically for most former Tory voters to get to. What the party needed was someone who could believably be a Tory themselves (Nick Clegg pre-2010, for instance), someone who could honestly say to this group of people: 'Hey, I'm just like you; a liberal, free market, free trade, pro-European. The Tories have abandoned that ground in search of UKIP voters – come join me instead.' Farron never tried this in earnest and wouldn't have been believed anyhow.

Going into the 2017 general election, then, the Lib Dems couldn't construct a coherent image beyond their stance on leaving the EU. The party was collectively scared to do anything that would genuinely alienate the left, due to that forlorn wish to regain votes from this end of the political spectrum – and most of the older parts of its membership base fit into the soft-left category I ascribed to Farron anyhow. As a result, the Lib Dems avoided coming to any big decisions on policies that would have been seen as too right or too left, resulting in a neither-here-nor-there manifesto that was far mushier than their (often unfairly maligned) 2015 offering. Thus, even those willing to look past Farron as leader couldn't find a believable way to the Lib Dems forming a realistic opposition to Brexit when they seemed to have no other policies – or at least, no policies on bread-and-butter issues. Most voters who really wanted to register a 'soft Brexit' vote thus went to Labour, as I have discussed already, even though on paper that made little sense given Labour's pro-hard Brexit positioning.

This all brings us to what is probably the main problem that held the Lib Dems back in the 2017 general election and will continue to do so in future unless the issue is addressed directly: they have what seems to be an unshakeable idea of themselves as a small party. They simply do not have what it takes to behave like a large party-in-waiting, and furthermore, they show no real signs other than through the occasional throwaway rhetoric that they have any desire to be anything other than what they are currently, which is a very esoteric debating society with a very small parliamentary wing.

Many political entities have been electorally decimated over the past twenty years, only to come back and even govern with parliamentary majorities again. The Conservatives in Canada, down at one point to a mere two seats nationwide, spring immediately to mind. But the Canuck Tories never lost their idea of themselves as a large party, a party of government, and thus were able to rebuild. The Lib Dems seem doomed because they cannot – more pertinently, *will not* – transform themselves into a large party-in-waiting.

Steven Tyler, the lead singer of Aerosmith, once talked about how the band would approach every gig they had in the very early days like they were the Rolling Stones playing Madison Square Garden. They faked being a big band until the day that they were, in other words. The Lib Dems just don't seem capable of the Aerosmith trick. Having experience within the party, I think I understand why.

For a political party in the UK, the Liberal Democrats are a very bottom-up organisation. It's why things like imposing all-women shortlists on constituencies has been so impossible to achieve; they are simply too local in terms of how they operate to allow the party leadership to impose its will. This results in diffuse thinking with a tendency to focus on niche issues (cannabis legalisation, electoral reform, sex workers) and an inability to reach consensus on the larger, trickier problems the country faces (take your pick). During Nick Clegg's time as leader, by sheer force of will and having a very good team around him, this limitation was navigated around as much as possible. However, this always caused friction within the party and mostly explains why the membership reasserted itself with such vigour post-2015, and furthermore why the leadership has been so supplicant to the activists in terms of the party's direction since Clegg stepped down as leader.

I'll touch briefly again here on the 'progressive alliance', but with specific reference to the Liberal Democrats this time: here they were, facing an election in which Labour were supposedly folding like a deck of cards and in which they could exploit that weakness to reel in Remainer votes. Yet their first instinct was to try to form some sort of loose alignment with Labour in order to halt the Tory onslaught. This is nonsensical behaviour if you are genuinely trying to overtake Labour as the natural rival to the Conservatives; perfectly understandable if you see yourselves as a small cog in a 'progressive' machine whose purpose is vague. On the morning of 9 June, Farron gave a rally-the-troops speech entitled 'Challenging the Conservative orthodoxy'. Throughout, he railed against the Tories, again and again, while Labour got one, very brief mention. This revealed Farron's (and most of the activist base's) deep desire to fight the Tories and no one else, and thus why the general election had not worked out as the party had hoped.

A huge problem not acknowledged enough was that the rise of the Liberal Democrats in the early part of the twenty-first century planted the seeds of the party's eventual downfall. During the Charles Kennedy leadership, the Lib Dems pitched themselves explicitly to the left of Blair's Labour on most issues; this reached its apex with the party's opposition to the Iraq invasion that had been undertaken by the New Labour government. In the build-up to the 2005 general election, the Lib Dems gained the votes of many young leftists wishing for an alternative to New Labour. This was the party's base going into the 2010 general election, when the leader was Nick Clegg. Nick's vision for the Liberal Democrats was the opposite of this in many ways, trying to make the Lib Dems a serious party of government as opposed to an outlet for outraged left-wingers. Unfortunately, the party ended up with an activist base that was largely composed of these leftists who had joined the party over Iraq; thus, when the Lib Dems went into coalition with the Tories, this all fell apart. To compound matters, Tim Farron then tried to take the party back to the Charles Kennedy era, only to find out that inevitably in a Britain in which the Labour Party had a properly left-wing leader and the Greens had managed to gain a much higher media profile than they had a decade ago, there were no votes left in that position for the Lib Dems.

So what, then, is the future of the Liberal Democrats? I think the 2017 general election has not only shown how damaged the party's brand is but also damaged it significantly further. Recovering all on its own is probably beyond its capabilities, particularly given the party's innate lack of ambition. Meanwhile, the realignment many of us may have hoped the election result would put on the table looks further away than ever as a result of Labour's better than expected showing. I suppose all the Lib Dems can do is keep on being the Lib Dems and hope for the best. Sort of a cruel fate, I guess, but at least most of the people inside the party will be happy with it.

PART II

A BRIEF BUT NECESSARY GLANCE AT THE LEFT'S RECENT HISTORY

CHAPTER 8

ED AND JEREMY

At the start of the coalition in 2010, Labour faced two parties telling the exact same story about the government that had preceded it: that New Labour had directly caused the hardships Britons faced in the wake of the 2008 financial crisis by having not 'mended the roof while the sun was shining'. The only way to have effectively combated this narrative would have been for Labour to have told their own version of what had led to the financial crash as well as how the actions the party took after it hit were essential in staving off the worst of what could have come the UK's way. In other words, to defend their record in government vigorously. Instead, Ed Miliband bizarrely reinforced the coalition's story about Labour's economic mismanagement by disavowing New Labour's time in government almost entirely himself. His reasons for doing this were mostly parochial: he had won the leadership contest by appealing to the left of his party, and he wanted to keep them on side by posing as someone who disliked New Labour almost as much as they did (despite having been both a special adviser and a minister in the government in question). This was astonishingly short-sighted, and kept Labour on the wrong side of an economic scrap they never had to lose.

Ed Miliband also compounded the problem in two ways. One, by joining the left in their retreat into navel-gazing by appearing at marches against austerity cuts, comparing the protestors to the suffragettes in one notable instance.* This cemented a version of political reality that, even after the 2015 general election, even after Brexit, and that only now, after the last election, is starting to thaw: the Tories were getting on with sorting out the mess that Labour left behind, while Labour itself threw an adolescent spat and talked only to itself. Miliband pursued at the same time what swiftly became known as the '35 per cent strategy'. A shorthand explanation of this strategy goes thus: do as little as possible

---

* Ed Miliband speech at a TUC anti-austerity rally in Hyde Park, London, 27 March 2011

and wait for the coalition to fall apart. If that doesn't happen before 2015, the Lib Dem vote from 2010 will all go to Labour and we'll win by default then anyhow. What is amazing about this plan of action, such as it was, is that anyone who had even a basic grasp of psephology could have told Miliband this was a terrible idea. Most of the seats held by the Lib Dems after the 2010 general election were Tory-facing; that is to say, they were seats in which the Conservatives had come second in recent elections and in which Labour were nowhere. It was blatantly obvious that a collapse in the Lib Dem vote could only have one result: a Tory majority – which is precisely what actually happened. Yet Miliband based an entire four-and-a-half-year stint as Leader of the Opposition on this exceptionally flawed premise.

Ed Miliband's most damaging intervention, however, was almost certainly the change he made to the way Labour elects its leaders, instituting a system whereby party members had the only say in the matter. Prior to this, Labour leaders were elected by thirds: one third of the vote came from trade unions, another third from the Parliamentary Labour Party, the other from the members. This system was itself a change from the way Labour had chosen its leaders between 1900 (the year the party was founded) and 1983, when the system of

thirds was established, which was that the only electorate that got to decide who would be the leader of the
party was the MPs. The PLP choosing the leader directly
makes the most sense when one comes to understand
the historic mission of the Labour Party: to maintain a
presence in Parliament in order to give the movement
the MPs represent a voice in the Commons – to which
end the very first clause of the Labour constitution is
dedicated. When Miliband changed the system, he not
only paved the way for Corbyn to become leader and for
there to be no way to remove Corbyn from the leadership even after 80 per cent of the PLP wanted him gone;
he changed the basic nature of the Labour Party itself by
effectively nullifying Clause One, which reads: organise
and maintain a political Labour Party in Parliament and
the country. The PLP is the Labour Party for all intents
and purposes; or at least, it was.

Corbyn's mistakes since becoming leader in September 2015 are many, despite the very recent reinvention of
his reputation as a truly great leader. The 2017 general
election campaign really papered over his faults, as for
once he played to his strengths: talking to people one
on one; demonstrating his long-held talent as a very,
very good constituency MP; speaking at the 'town hall'
style television events; putting on display his general
strengths as a campaigner. It will be interesting to see

if he can maintain the cuddly media persona he managed to create during the campaign, or if grouchy, irate Corbyn makes a return.

Despite the relatively good general election result, in context, Corbyn's leadership skills remain suspect at best. Worth noting is his contempt for parliamentary democracy (his disdain for the Labour MPs who do not agree with him fully; his lackadaisical approach to House proceedings), coupled with his worship of South American-style street movements (his recently well-noted support for the Venezuelan regime under both Chávez and Maduro), none of which bodes well in a prospective Prime Minister. He also naively believes that he can inspire a quasi-revolution in Britain by turning Labour into a movement – again, the exact opposite reason the Labour Party was founded in 1900, which was to take social movements and give them a voice in Parliament. These problems remain extremely relevant to the future of the party, particularly now that Corbyn and his wing have unquestionable control of it, at least for the foreseeable future.

All of this has made the situation of the Labour moderates within the Parliamentary Labour Party much worse than it was before the general election. This, oddly, could be the lasting legacy of Theresa May's presumably brief premiership: the destruction of the Labour Party, albeit by completely different means than she would ever have envisioned and with her, bizarrely, as one of the victims of it all. With Corbyn and his brand of leftism entrenched within Labour now, it may be that the moderates will need to either break off and form a new centrist party or admit that they were wrong and follow Corbyn. Otherwise, what is the point in staying in politics? The problem with the former solution is that they have just had the enduring appeal of the Labour brand demonstrated to them in the most dramatic way imaginable. What do they do now, then? We'll park that for now, but later in the book I will examine these possibilities in depth.

Two leaders of the Labour Party, both of them very different in certain ways but also with many more similarities. Both of them lost elections on soft-left manifestos, yet one was internally considered a crushing failure due to the expectation beforehand of a win (or at least, of being the biggest party), the other considered a massive success due to the expectation beforehand of a historic, crushing defeat as opposed to a run-of-the-mill one.

The sharp decline of the centre left in Britain over the past decade, from the dominant force in British politics three elections running to a place where being sixty-odd seats short of a majority is hailed as a massive triumph, cannot entirely be laid at the feet of Ed Miliband and

Jeremy Corbyn. More significant are the factors which led those two individuals to become leaders of the Labour Party in the first place; a complex series of social and political stories stretching back several decades.

CHAPTER 9

HOW THE CENTRE HAS HELD
– BUT MAY NOT HOLD MUCH LONGER

Labour has always been a large coalition of not com-pletely comfortable bedfellows, right from around the time it displaced the Liberal Party as the main opposi-tion to the Tories. For the greater part of a century, these cracks were papered over effectively by the party most of the time. There were moments when the differences between factions within the Labour fold became visi-bly difficult – the early 1980s, with the problems which led to the creation of the SDP, springing immediately to mind – but for most of Labour's history, the centre has held. Over the past decade, however, it has become increasingly impossible for the party to reach out to the same voters that caused it to win in 1997, 2001 and 2005, and this was still a problem in 2017. Many on the hard left have a point when they say that many left-wing policies are now popular, and that the country is ripe for an anti-austerity party to govern it, yet winning a majority still requires Labour to win the kinds of seats it won in those three aforementioned victories, and the result of the previous general election offers little comfort in this regard.

What is interesting about the Labour decline since 2010 is how slow it has been. We see a great 'stickiness' in the Labour vote asserting itself time and again, showing itself with a vengeance in June 2017. During the 2010 general election campaign, after Cleggmania and the resulting poll bounce for the Liberal Democrats, there was panic within the Labour leadership, sparked by a worry that not only would they lose that election but possibly not even form the official opposition afterwards either. In the end, particularly given the poor quality of Labour's election campaign coming at the end of thirteen years of Labour government, 258 seats seemed a bad result but not as bad as it could have been. There exists a deep, tribal loyalty to the Labour Party across parts of England and Wales that has proven more difficult to break down than many would have foreseen.

Yet despite the unquestionable ability of Labour's brand to attract more voters than expected, as witnessed during the decade leading up to the 2017 general election, no political party, however supposedly secure its brand, can continue to fight against reality. The poor choice of leadership, which I covered in the previous chapter, undoubtedly played a massive role in Labour going from the 2005 majority in which they held 355 seats to the current 262 seats it holds today. However, even had the party picked much, much better people to steer the ship, they would have faced unavoidable difficulties in trying to win another election after the 2005 poll. Some of these problems are common to all (or at least, almost all) centre-left parties throughout the Western world post-2008; others are unique to the British Labour Party.

The ones which afflict centre-left parties generally have to do with the very deep divide between urban professionals and their supporting immigrant populations on the one hand, and those rooted to one particular place, who find themselves further and further removed from the active portions of the economy, on the other. To study the first half of this equation: Londoners voted strongly to Remain in the European Union; it was 60/40 in favour of remaining in the EU across the capital, and that figure takes into account the much more Brexit-favourable suburbs (many central London boroughs voted over 70 per cent Remain). The reasons for this are usually lazily drifted past, but the stark difference in how

London voted in the referendum compared with the rest of the country gets to the heart of the main long-term problem the centre left faces.

The well-paid urban professionals with mortgages and houses accruing value, the young professionals living on cereal and sleeping in bedsits, and the immigrants existing on even less food and in even worse conditions than the youthful native workers all, oddly, share an entire set of both identifiable values and economic interests. To put it more succinctly, they like the system pretty much as it is, although possibly with more public spending involved in some cases. The well-paid for obvious reasons; the young up-and-comers because they see themselves as being amongst the well-paid at some point in the relatively near future; the immigrant population because the lives they live in London are infinitely superior to the ones they left behind in their countries of birth. All of these groups love London's vibrancy and excitement; all of them feel instinctively international and thus usually pro-EU; all of them have a place in an ecosystem that they at the very least feel is the best possible one for them to be in at present.

This is why Labour still does so well in London; the party not only managed to gain seats in the capital during the 2017 general election, they put most of their existing majorities up into third-world dictatorship territory, getting 80 per cent of the vote in some constituencies. This success has come despite Labour having backed the triggering of Article 50 with no resistance and inviting in a supposed threat from the Liberal Democrats as a result. Labour has managed to increase its reach into this metropolitan group, with the diminishing of the Lib Dem vote being a helpful factor in this regard in spite of these problems.

As far as the 2017 general election went, the Labour vote held up in the north of England in a way that was unexpected. However, the results were strange in many ways, reflecting a still hard-to-read result: the Tories gained Mansfield in Nottinghamshire, a Labour seat since 1923, as well as Middlesbrough and East Cleveland, another long-held Labour constituency, both of those results cutting against the grain of the 'brilliant defeat' narrative. Labour's vote was patchy, in other words.

The better than expected election result for Labour obscures the fact that they still have major problems with large sections of their core vote. Many may have turned out to vote Labour this time round, having suddenly fallen out of love with Theresa May, but that doesn't mean that these voters are solidly back in the fold either. Most of the items in the Labour manifesto played strongly to what is their new base, the urban troika I discussed earlier, as opposed to the old one: free childcare, free tuition fees and – in a direct attack on the Tories main core vote – a guarantee on the triple pensions lock. Labour are still without a lot to say to the working classes, other than that they will end austerity (which, admittedly, if the Tories continue under weak leadership, may be enough). As I say, working-class voters may not have been taken in by Theresa May's empty rhetoric either, but this vote is still very vulnerable, and if the Tories could find a way to reach this target audience as they threatened to pre-manifesto launch, then there's your Conservative landslide for you.

Most of these problems, as I mentioned, are shared by other traditional parties of the centre left throughout Europe. However, unique to the British Labour Party has been the 'toys out of the pram' movement of direction since losing power in 2010. Faced with the choice of either dealing with the fact that new solutions are required to deal with the problems of the twenty-first century or retreating into a comforting shell, the left has chosen the latter, partially after 2010, almost fully following the 2015 defeat, and completely after 2017.

Another, bigger dilemma that Labour faces that other centre-left parties in Europe do not (simply because they faced down this pivotal problem a generation ago) is what do with socialism itself. It has been clear since at least the fall of the Berlin Wall that most Western societies will never, ever countenance the notion of electing a properly socialist party, and by this I want to specify that I do mean socialism in the truest ideological sense of the term – involving the desire to nationalise as much of the economy as possible, as quickly as possible. This explicitly does not mean that a very left-wing socially democratic party cannot gain power in Britain; it is one of the central pillars of this entire book that a socially democratic party, so long as it had certain things going for it, could indeed gain a parliamentary majority.

Socialism was attempted as an experiment across the world during the twentieth century, and every time it was not only a disaster but a very similar-looking disaster; remarkable given the cultural disparities involved across all of the countries in which it was tried out as an economic system. In fact, one of the reasons that the centre left was so successful in the 1990s, the era immediately following the fall of European socialism, was that it openly renounced socialism and embraced social democracy instead – although in Britain this was fudged, with Blair's controversial redrafting of Clause IV of the Labour constitution actually leaving the word 'socialism' in the body of the text. Most of the European centre left openly accepted not only that the free market was here to stay but that this wasn't actually a bad thing; furthermore, that redistribution via state mechanisms could fruitfully take place against the backdrop of bourgeois liberal democracy. This obvious acceptance at a deep level, not just rhetorical but emotional as well, helped the European left to gain power across most of the Continent during the decade following the collapse of the Soviet Union.

The 2008 financial crash ruined this for the left in that it seemed to blow a hole in the Third Way – the economic and political theory that there was something between social democracy and neoliberalism. As long as spending on public services remained high but personal taxes relatively low, people bought into the idea that taxes could be kept low because the Western economy, shorn of the vagaries of history at long last, would grow at a steady pace for the rest of eternity, with the days of 'boom and bust' supposedly gone for ever. However, once the centre right told the public that the centre left had been wrong about this and that reliance on these ideas had led directly to the 2008 crash (not really strictly true, but with enough of a patina of reality to wash), the left needed to come up with a counter-narrative. It failed miserably to do so. On one hand, cuts and 'austerity' were derided as misjudgements on the part of the ruling right; on the other, when pressed on whether they would raise taxes to keep public spending high, the British left invariably fudged the answer. Maybe. Probably. Probably not. Yes, we'd cut, but they would somehow be nicer cuts than the cuts the right are currently making.

In the midst of this confusion about what the centre left stood for and why people should vote for it, the hard left spotted an opportunity and ran with it. In the same way that the hard right rose in the same period of time because they at least had an easy-to-understand answer to the world's ills (just kick the foreigners out and everything will be rosy), the hard left told us all that 'socialism' was the answer. What defined socialism, however, was usually anyone's guess. Often times it was something weirdly akin to Harold Macmillan-style, 1950s wet Toryism; on other occasions, it was talking up the notion that 'post-capitalism' was imminent and that when it hit, people would huddle towards the left for warmth (despite specific evidence to the contrary, namely the immediate aftermath of the 2008 financial crash itself).

The 2017 general election certainly didn't demonstrate that Britain is willing to elect a socialist government, particularly considering a very non-socialist government was the one that actually emerged from the poll as the government. It did show that many people were irritated enough with the status quo to vote for Labour in protest, but there is no reason to believe that Britain as a whole is any readier to elect a socialist government now than it was in 1983. Given that for the foreseeable future Labour is now stuck with a leadership that in its heart of hearts wishes to be as socialist as possible, this could present a problem for them.

CHAPTER 10

LABOUR CONFERENCE, 2016: LIVERPOOL TRANSFORMED

For a reasonable length of time, Labour conference was the largest gathering of centre-left individuals anywhere on the continent of Europe every single year. Those days are sadly gone. The last time it felt really huge was 2010, the year Labour crashed out of government after thirteen years. It occurred only four months after the general election that had resulted in the first Labour defeat since 1992, but already the New Labour era felt distant. In spite of that, half of central Manchester was walled off to host the event; the helicopters still buzzed overhead as they had in years past; the whole thing still felt massive. As Ed Miliband narrowly beat his brother to the leadership, Labour expected to be back in power soon enough – maybe even in as little as a year or so if the coalition government fell to pieces over the AV referendum, something that seemed palpably possible in September 2010.

Since then, each Labour Party conference has felt slightly smaller than the one that preceded it. I remember 2014, again in Manchester, having watched Ed Miliband give the worst speech I've ever seen any major political figure give in the history of the human race (to jog your memory, it was the one that started with twenty minutes of anecdotes involving Ed wandering around posh bits of north London and having random conversations with people named Gareth). I proceeded to the Midland Hotel's bar that evening only to find a gaggle of researchers getting leathered, laughing wildly as if the apocalypse were mere hours away; they had held dreams of being departmental spads that very morning still, but after that speech any remaining hopes of such a possibility had been dashed to the winds.

I recall 2015 in Brighton, Corbyn's leadership having barely begun, standing in the exhibition hall just as John McDonnell gave his speech. While he namechecked a list of major corporations who were all apparently evil in some respect, the people manning the stalls representing those organisations made panicked phone calls to home base. Amongst the things I was quick to discover as I walked around the ACC Liverpool a year later was the fact that none of those same corporations had bothered to turn up that year. The exhibition hall looked and felt like something familiar to those of us who have attended many Lib Dem conferences: a lot of internal organisations, such as 'Labour Friends of [insert country or ideology here]'. In fact, it was pretty much exactly a Lib Dem-style exhibition hall, save for the strong trade union contingent.

There was a lot more to notice at the 2016 Labour conference if you were a veteran of these sorts of things. As I say, every one of them since 2010 had seemed increasingly less significant and less well attended; 2016's edition made a rather epic leap in that direction, however. Even more so than 2015, Labour conference 2016 reminded me on first impression of the Lib Dems'; specifically, it reminded me of the Lib Dem spring conference of 2015 in the same location. Coming as it did at the tired fag-end of the coalition years, with a handful of ageing activists rattling around the oversized building, it called to attention at every step the inevitable loss of seats and the loss of significance to follow. The security in Liverpool was actually the first thing that brought all this to one's attention at the Labour conference in 2016; gone was the heavy security that attends serious political party gatherings in Britain, replaced by a Lib Dem-esque system of blokes in security jackets nonchalantly inspecting delegate badges.

In addition to the exhibition hall having been cleared of paying corporate clients and the security being significantly toned down, the 'travelling circus' that attends conference – lobbyists, the media, relevant NGO groups – was notably thin on the ground too. I suppose the Corbynites thought that was wonderful, being very pure and all of that, but it gave an outsider such as myself the distinct impression of Labour going down in the world. Clearly, fewer people thought coming to Labour conference was worth the time and effort, given the possibility of the party coming to power was so tiny, and perception is not without importance in politics, to put it mildly.

Not that there were Corbynites in large numbers within the confines of the Liverpool ACC either, for they had decamped to their own, separate conference (although they claimed that it wasn't a conference but rather a sort of 'festival'), organised by (who else?) Momentum (the organisation whose raison d'être is to support Corbyn's leadership of the Labour Party), a brisk walk away from the main conference in Liverpool as well. 'The World Transformed', they called it, without apparent irony. I had thought to avoid the Momentum sideshow completely before I'd headed north; to simply concentrate on what I had come to Labour conference to achieve (which was to attend some fringe events and dinners, but mostly to do what I do every year, which was to wander around and note the increased chaos and diminished attendance). However, once I was at the funeral that was the main Labour conference, the Momentum 'festival' seemed too good to miss, so I decided to brave the sharp breeze off the Mersey and walk up into town to check it out.

It was much as I had expected beforehand. Stalls selling or giving away Corbyn-themed tat were everywhere, and if you had been away from British politics completely for a few years and knew nothing whatsoever about what had gone on in your absence, you would have descended on the Black-E (a fantastic venue, incidentally) convinced that Jeremy Corbyn had died and been canonised by the left for some heroic feat he had performed. It is easy to take the piss out of something like The World Transformed, and many have already done so, thus I'll spare you further on that front; suffice it to say, the overwhelming feeling I got from wandering around the place was sadness. Like watching lemmings running towards the cliff's edge and wanting to save the poor little things but realising there's no way to do so; you must simply watch nature run its course. I didn't stay at The World Transformed very long, preferring even the death-warmed-up feel of the actual conference to the horrors of witnessing the left's supernova.

As I returned to the main conference venue, I scouted the bar, saw no familiar faces (there were about five people in there at the time), and then scanned the programme guide to alight on the fact that the London Labour drinks reception was just about to start. Gold, thought I, at least the London reception should be happening, given the capital is the one last bastion of reliable Labouriness.

When I walked into the reception, I figured I must have made an error in regards to location; the room was half full. Sure, it was still early, but in years past this was the gig you had to show up for bang on time lest you find yourself unable to squeeze in. The few souls who had braved it talked grumpily amongst themselves about the demise of the Labour Party as well as how shit conference that year was shaping up to be. There was far more of an anti-Corbyn vibe in the air than I would have ever expected. At least the lack of bodies meant a surplus of food, so I decided to make my way to the buffet. While scooping some houmous onto my plate, I heard the unmistakable sound of Jeremy Corbyn's voice. It sounded weak and processed, so my first thought was: 'Why are they pumping old Corbyn speeches through the speakers?', a hypothesis that was quickly destroyed as I turned around to see the leader of the Labour Party himself standing mere feet away from me. He had started giving a speech and was being studiously ignored by almost everyone in the room. Several of the people standing within cat-swinging distance from the dear leader had their backs turned to him, as if he wasn't there at all. It was like it was the ghost of Corbyn coming back to haunt London activists, as opposed to the actual living human being, and somehow only I could see him and he was ignoring me for having been so mean about him so often.

It was mercifully soon over, and when he got to the end of what he had to say, Corbyn simply turned around and walked out of the room with zero fanfare. It remains one of the most surreal things I've ever experienced in British politics. After all that, I found myself back in the bar (it having warmed up a little in the interim) speaking to some friends of mine whom one could classify as mild Corbyn supporters. I told them about the weird Corbyn speech I had just been witness to.

'Yeah, that is a problem with Jeremy. He can be really boring to listen to sometimes,' said one. This was too plaintive, however, and several of the others jumped to the dear leader's defence.

'Jeremy's not boring! He's complex. It's like listening to John Coltrane – the first time you hear it, it's like noise you can't get your brain around. You have to give it a chance for the nuances to sink in – when you do, it's amazing, and you wonder how you could have ever listened to the crap pop music you liked before.'

After having an involuntary shiver at the idea of Trane being likened to Jeremy Corbyn, I asked what kind of crap pop music Ed Miliband had been. The one who had made the Coltrane comparison declined to comment, but my friend who had made the admission that Corbyn was dull had this to say: 'Ed was like the songs buried in the middle of an Orchestral Manoeuvres in the Dark LP. Sort of trying to be too complicated and lyrically deep for its own good, but still managing to be cheesy somehow in the end anyhow.'

'I don't want to be in a party with Jeremy fucking Corbyn,' a member of the commentariat said, and I instantly wished I had that exact slogan printed on a T-shirt. A Labour peer, one of Gordon Brown's old advisors, was more zen about the whole thing.

'Bad leaders come and go. The Labour Party will survive, somehow. We'll rise again.'

The following morning, I was up early to do a BBC TV spot on the theme of 'What now for the Labour Party after the second leadership contest victory for the Corbmeister'. I was tired and not in the mood for it and, faced with interminably dull questions from the host, I mumbled my way through it all. What was there really to say about it anyway?

Next up, I had to chair a fringe event on the future of trade unions. I had written on the subject recently and the fringe panel had on it Gavin Kelly, the old head of policy under Brown who had gone on to lead the Resolution Foundation; John Hannett, the general secretary of Usdaw (the Union of Shop, Distributive and Allied Workers); Frances O'Grady, the general secretary of the TUC (Trades Union Congress); Polly Toynbee, the *Guardian* columnist, and Stephen Kinnock, Labour MP for Aberavon. My take on the future of trade unionism was that the Len McCluskey approach of wanting as much nationalisation as possible was foolhardy and outdated; that trade unions had to learn from their Nordic cousins how to grow their memberships to the point where they were too large to be ignored. The talk at the fringe was rather painful. Not amongst the panel, who were all very eloquent on the topic (although Polly grated on me a little with her nostalgia for the 1970s, which I thought was somewhat unfortunate), but rather when we went to comments and questions from the crowd. Other than a few lobbyist NGO types, everyone said that trade unions needed to fight for a fully socialist Britain; that any concessions to the free market system were ill-advised and should be avoided.

That evening I went to dinner with some Labour MPs and a few people who had worked for Ed Miliband when he was leader who were now working mostly in the private sector. I brought up an article that I had written recently about how now was probably the time for the moderates to split and form their own party, and that they may look back with regret if they didn't do so only to have to face a possible general election in 2017, when they would be forced to tell people on the doorstep that they wanted Corbyn to be Prime Minister (or so I figured at the time). I'll never forget what one of the north-east MPs had to say:

> We're not going to hand the far left the Labour Party to keep. I'm not going anywhere – this was my grandfather's party, my father's party, and it's my party. I shouldn't have to leave my own party to accommodate some out-of-touch liberal London cabal. It's them that should split off and start their own thing, not us lot.

While I could see his point, I could also see that for mostly unfair reasons, the far left really *had* succeeded in kidnapping the Labour Party, and that was that.

I spent the next morning away from conference, just soaking up Liverpool. My father is a Scouser and so I always enjoy returning to the city, even if I only do so sparingly (or when work happens to take me there). I wandered around the Tate a little, letting the depressing, fading spectacle that the Labour Party had descended into wash away from me. After a brief stroll along Mathew Street, I walked to Lime Street Station and headed back to London, glad to be putting Labour conference behind me for another year.

There is something perverse about the idea of the hard left finally gaining control of the Labour Party, only to turn around and run a separate conference at the same time and in the same city, allowing the official conference to rot. The fact that Momentum plan to do the exact same thing in Brighton in 2017 shows that they understand fully what they are doing – without understanding the full consequences of what they are summoning forth, and the negative effects it is bound to have on causes they hold dear.

CHAPTER 11

SADIQ KHAN: THE BRITISH LEFT'S ONE REAL VICTORY IN RECENT MEMORY

Months out from the 2016 London mayoral election, I was a genuine swing voter. I had gone for Boris Johnson in 2012 by default – I couldn't vote for Ken, since one of my few absolutely hard rules in approaching any plebiscite is that I never, ever put an X next to the name of anyone who publicly supports a fascist dictatorship. Livingstone's open admiration for Hugo Chávez more than qualified under this provision, and so I held my nose and voted for Mr Anti-Bendy Buses. In 2016, there was nothing of that nature to consider, so I was going to let the campaigns help me decide.

Right after Zac Goldsmith had received the Conservative nomination, I bumped into one of Sadiq's lieutenants, an old acquaintance of mine, on the Tube.

'The Tories are going to make this all about Sadiq being a Muslim. They will try to make him out to be some kind of Islamic extremist.'

I disagreed heartily. I said I thought that Zac's campaign would steer well clear of anything religious, as that would be a terrible idea. Instead, it would attack Sadiq's links with the trade unions, with the Tories implying that if he were mayor it would be a never-ending series of strikes on the public transportation system with the Labour mayor nodding along in agreement. It would also presumably try to paint Sadiq as a machine politician; uninventive and lacking in any new and bold ideas, as against Zac the Maverick.

Turns out I was wrong and my friend who works for Sadiq was correct. I was right in one respect: going after Sadiq on the grounds of his religion was indeed a terrible idea. The Goldsmith campaign's decision to try to stitch Khan up as an extremist backfired very, very badly. Many assume that is why Sadiq won. However, I think there was more to it than that, and the reasons he became the first Muslim mayor of London are instructive for progressives of every, any and no party allegiance.

First of all, Sadiq seemed to have a plan for running

London, one that was progressive without being overly radical and thus scary, and most of all, one that sounded affordable. John McDonnell (and, to be fair, Ed Balls to some extent before him) is obsessed with wanting all of Labour's plans to be costed, but the truth is, the most important thing is for the plans in question to sound like they have been really thought through. As Labour found out in the 2017 general election campaign, there is no point in costing everything correctly only to then have your spokespeople go on media outlets not knowing or understanding the relevant figures. If you sound like you know what you're talking about, people are inclined to believe you. There is a cod philosophy in Westminster that Labour spokespeople need to be more up on their figures than the corresponding Tories do; that the Conservative Party is given more leeway on financial issues since they have a better image in this regard with the general public. While this is partially true, the left always overplays this; Sadiq Khan's mayoral campaign demonstrates that if Labour runs a campaign in which it knows what it is talking about and has spokespeople who sound like they know what they are talking about in regards to financial matters, they can overcome this supposed prejudice that exists against Labour electorally.

In a similar vein, Sadiq's 2016 campaign for the London mayoralty was notable because he managed to project an image as someone who wanted to get things done; a politician who was a pragmatist first and foremost. Most left-wing political figures these days feel the need to present themselves as doctrinaires, first and foremost. This is usually a huge error, as most people tend to read in ideology when a politician is of the left, even if a politician isn't trying to talk up any particular ideological bent. In other words, the public tends to hear ideology in everything a left-wing politician says, so anything whispered sounds spoken, anything spoken sounds shouted, and anything shouted sounds as if it has been belllowed through a megaphone when it comes to matters of doctrine. Politicians of the left don't need to convince the electorate that they mean well or that they have deeply felt convictions; that is taken as read, even when it is objectively highly questionable (as witnessed in the most recent general election, when the Tories' IRA-related attacks on Corbyn failed to stick). What left-wing politicians need to do is convince voters that they are more concerned with fixing the problems as perceived, and that they will do so in a straightforward, effective manner.

Sadiq managed a trick that will be vital for Corbyn to learn from if he really wants to win that parliamentary majority he missed out on last time: he will have to appeal to centrist, swing voters, people who will have voted Tory at recent elections (there is no way Sadiq would have won if he couldn't have convinced a substantial number of people who had voted for Boris Johnson in 2012 to vote for him in 2016) – while also retaining the young, left-of-centre vote at the same time, on the same platform. Sadiq managed to do it in London. One wonders if Sadiq could have won the 2017 general election with the same trick had he been leader of the Labour Party at the time – it is worth bearing in mind that he got 57 per cent of the vote. We'll never know.

PART III

THE LEFT'S STRUCTURAL PROBLEMS EXAMINED

CHAPTER 12

WHY WE'RE STUCK WITH CAPITALISM – OR SOMETHING INFINITELY WORSE

Even trying to define what makes one left-wing as opposed to fitting into another political description these days is surprisingly difficult. Most people on the left aren't even really socialists any more, as I discussed in Part II. Being of the left in 2017 amounts to little more than an elaborate pose, as far as I can tell, built around a professed desire to strike against the 'establishment' whenever possible. Given that the left wants the state to do more not less, this cry against the 'establishment' that they always struggle to really define is problematic as an ideological rallying cry; they don't really want to tear down the establishment at all – they just want to become it themselves.

Having thought about it in depth, here is what I think it really means to be of the left these days. It is to believe that these three propositions are not only true, but essential:

1. Capitalism is BAD and we need something to replace it as an economic system (although Soviet-style socialism is BAD too, there is some abstract version of socialism no one can define as yet that is GOOD).
2. We need to come up with something quickly, though, because capitalism is in its final, decadent phase and will fall apart sometime soon (how soon is never specified, but believe us, it will be SOON).
3. This collapse of capitalism that is approaching will be a bona fide GOOD THING, because even though we have no idea what will replace it, we take it as an article of faith that it will be much better than capitalism and, furthermore, that the collapse itself will be GOOD because it will finally force whatever shape the post-capitalist economy is supposed to take to do so by default.

I disagree with all three of these statements myself, as do most reasonable people who have ever defined as centre left in the past two decades at least (although few will want to publicly admit it now, post-general election surge). Deconstructing why I think they are incorrect leads us to why I think the left has so many deep, structural problems, and why these conundrums will continue to make Labour far less electable than it otherwise would be.

Let's start at the top. Listing the problems that capitalism has at present isn't all that difficult, and only free market purists would disagree with most of what I'm about to say. It has a tendency to create monopolies, so that even the advantages of capitalism get cancelled out in the process – this is one of the reasons that rail nationalisation is a popular policy, for instance. It is not down to socialist orthodoxy: people are trapped in a broken market and figure that at least if the government ran the trains again, the rail-going public would have the threat of succession in the form of the ballot box as a means of driving the service to be better, whereas now they have nothing at all. They cannot switch to another provider, nor can they find an alternate means of travel that is sufficient, so the private rail companies have no real pressure to make their services either better or cheaper.

When capitalism gets itself involved in markets where the demand is inelastic, like healthcare, it tends to create a horrible mess. Yet the harsh truth is that no other economic system that has ever been attempted at large scale across the whole of human history has ever actually even functioned let alone flourished. When capitalism is put in place after another, unfunctional system has been removed, even taking into account all of capitalism's downsides that I've discussed above, standards of living improve across the whole of the population, and the ranks of the middle classes swell as people formerly of the lower socio-economic classes prosper. China is only the largest case in point over the past half-century.

The left in Britain has only succeeded when it has embraced the fact that capitalism is necessary but flawed, and that the only way to even out the flaws is through some level of social democracy. Thus, by rejecting capitalism completely as it seems to want to do now, the left is cutting off its most saleable feature, which is a plan to make capitalism much better for most people.

Dealing next with the second statement, that capitalism is in its final, dying breaths: there is absolutely no evidence for this being the case and, in fact, plenty of evidence to the contrary. True, capitalism's triumph over communism in the late 1980s/early 1990s did not lead automatically to a democratic hegemony, as many naively anticipated; with hindsight, the Chinese and Russian models of crony capitalism with autocratic underpinnings were inevitable. However, recent history has weirdly proven all the more how adaptable and indispensable capitalism itself is. The despotic regimes of the old Second World did not want to give up their power after the fall of the Berlin Wall, and some found that by accepting capitalism they did not need to do so, as the prosperity brought by a capitalist economic system ended up propping them up in perpetuity. If anything, while liberal democracy looks increasingly shaky these days, capitalism appears to be even more hegemonic than ever. Liberal democracy is, it turns out, quite fragile, while capitalism is unbelievably adaptable, beyond what even its most vocal adherents after the fall of communism would have asserted.

Of course, in order to back up their theory that capitalism is reaching its end of days, some leftists point to the hypothesis that an economic crisis is coming our way, one that will be on par with 2008 or worse, and that it will destroy capitalism once and for all. Yet we already went through all that, in 2008 as it happens, and, while it was rocky, capitalism came out of it stronger, not weaker. The system didn't crumble, and there is no reason to think another crash would cause us to take up a completely different economic system. Why does the left think the response would vary greatly from the one rolled out in 2008, namely that the taxpayer would prop up the system and everyone would just muddle through? What realistic alternative do they imagine there is?

Taking on the third and final plank of the modern left: the idea that capitalism collapsing would be a good thing for anyone, but particularly for the poorest and most vulnerable in society, is naïve beyond description. Were capitalism to actually suffer some crisis beyond our current imagination and 'collapse', this would mean that society would almost certainly collapse as well, and by that I mean the basic systems via which we run our lives would be so deeply affected that faith in the monetary system would disappear and anarchy would descend. Violence would fill the void and soon enough it would be the strongest against the weakest, with predictable results. While the richest individuals in the old order would suffer a little by their money becoming worthless, they also have real assets, the most important being land, which would then be instantly invaluable. People with no assets would become the equivalent of willing slaves simply to live under the protection of the wealthy. Some would attempt to live in anarcho-syndicalist communes, no doubt, but they would only be able to last in this lifestyle if they were able to physically repel roving bandits by force.

If the *Mad Max*-style post-apocalyptic world I've just painted sounds far-fetched, I fail to see what else the collapse of the basic economic system we all live under would bring with it, particularly as the left openly has no system, even in theory, to replace it with. What else could emerge but violent anarchy? History tells us it's the only thing that would result if the system really did fall to pieces so quickly and dramatically.

To summarise: the thesis that capitalism is nearing its final implosion has no merit, and even if it did, it would only mean that the left were cheering on the destruction of the poorest and most vulnerable in society. This, as much as anything else I've covered so far, is how the left is continuing the process of moving away from, not towards, a real alternative to the Tory vision of Great Britain. Handouts to the middle class may get the Labour Party thirty-odd seats – hell, I'm willing to grant that if the Conservatives ran a campaign of equally poor quality again, the bungs might even get Labour a majority for a single parliament – but there is no genuine vision there for how we should deal with the challenges we face today, never mind the terrifying complexity of the future. This is the left's key flaw, for, beyond what it does to them electorally, it means that even if they got into power they wouldn't really know what to do with it.

CHAPTER 13

THE DREADED MAINSTREAM MEDIA AND THE LEFT

Rupert Murdoch will be furious when he finds out how many Sun readers voted Labour, reads a headline from The Canary, the mouthpiece for the British hard left.[*] To answer the obvious question that will spring into your mind, not very many *Sun* readers voted Labour (30 per cent) as it happens, but apparently the media mogul will still be apoplectic about it all anyhow. This article is a great example of a strain of modern leftist thinking, namely that the 'mainstream media' or MSM for short, is conspiring against the Labour Party constantly and

---

[*] Steve Topple, article on the Canary website, 14 June 2017, accessed 7 August 2017 at https://www.thecanary.co/2017/06/14/rupert-murdoch-will-abso-lutely-furious-finds-many-sun-readers-voted-labour-images/

that they are doing so to some nefarious end never really explained, apparently on account of it being so obvious to adherents of the left. What was actually missing from the Canary piece in question that you might usually see in an article of its type was a call for the press to be 'regulated' in order to root out 'bias', a common rallying call on the left, demonstrating one of the strangest turns the British left has made over the past decade: its revolt against freedom of speech. This isn't strictly a British problem, to be fair, as the American and continental European left have shown a similar tendency during the same period, but it is particularly virulent in Britain.

I could point to any number of examples of this be-haviour – John McDonnell telling the press to ask only questions scripted by the Labour Party during one par-ticularly awful 2017 election campaign press conference stands out – but I'll start with the most organised and pronounced amongst them. The Hacked Off campaign, which led to the Leveson Inquiry, is a good place to begin.

The essence of the Hacked Off campaign, as organised by ex-Lib Dem MP Evan Harris and taking as its figure-head the film actor Hugh Grant, is that the British press has too much freedom to do as it pleases and so we need a new set of laws to rein them in. It very effectively used the phone-hacking scandal to propel the campaign for-ward, particularly the gruesome Milly Dowler episode, using it as an example of why extra press regulation was essential. There was one rather large problem with this, however: all of the wrongdoings committed during the phone-hacking scandal were illegal already, and some people even went to prison for breaking those already existing laws, so one wonders how extra legislation being in place could have further prevented those misdeeds from happening.

I worked with some of the activists most passionate about press regulation about five years ago, while the Leveson stuff was in full swing.

'What we need is to nationalise all press in this country,' the most vocal amongst them told me one day. She was within earshot of a few of the others, who all looked uncomfortable with the idea of bringing all news in Britain under the aegis of the government, but said nothing to counter the impression that they intended to regulate the British press using Soviet-style methods. I asked her about what that would look like – and would it apply to bloggers?

'It would apply to everyone.'

I pointed out that, as an avid blogger, she herself would be silenced by her own proposals. She laughed a little at this suggestion and said: 'It wouldn't be opinions like mine that would need to be silenced under *the new way*.'

I'd like to stress here that the Hacked Off campaign never pursued such a harsh line on press regulation itself. Yet that was where the calls for Leveson 2 have ended up (the report on Leveson 1 was released on 29 November 2012; Leveson 2 has been dropped under the Tories), with many on the left seeing it not as a way to prevent something like the Milly Dowler hacking scandal from ever happening again, but rather to clamp down on freedom of the press because they keep using said freedom to be mean to Jeremy Corbyn. Hacked Off was at least an organised, professional campaign that tried to walk the line between press regulation and freedom of speech in a way that, while I disagreed with it, at least had a considered point to make. Since then, the attacks on freedom of speech from the left have grown more vocal and yet more chaotic at the same time. The consistent (and consistently irritating and unpleasant) attacks on the BBC News political editor Laura Kuenssberg is another good example of this behaviour.

It is worth pointing out that Laura Kuenssberg is the first woman to hold the position of political editor of BBC News, a fact that you would think the left would wish to celebrate, at least a little. Instead, she has been vilified as a 'Tory' (which, to be fair, in the Corbyn era means little more when uttered by a Corbynite than 'not in thrall to Corbyn') for what amounts to two things, as far as I can see it: one, doing her job and being critical of the Labour front bench when they mess up, which has been very often; two, for a particular incident from January 2016 in which Stephen Doughty, a Labour MP, resigned his shadow ministerial post live on the BBC. Afterwards, Seumas Milne, Labour's director of communications, complained to the BBC about the interview. Apparently, Labour objected to the idea of the BBC having a shadow minister resign on air without party HQ having been given the heads up beforehand. Nor were they just unhappy about this development (indeed, it would be strange if they had not been); rather, they thought that the BBC had acted improperly in some definable way; that they had stepped outside of their remit as a publicly owned body. There is an element of wishing to control the press in this incident that should make any liberal feel very uncomfortable, whatever your particular views on Laura Kuenssberg's supposed political opinions.

One of the reasons Hacked Off and the Laura Kuenssberg hounding have fallen into the mainstream of left-wing politics in Britain is a partly understandable anger at the way the right-of-centre media in Britain operates. The right sells more newspapers than the left (although the gulf is not as large as many on the left think it is). The *Daily Mail* is far and away the most popular newspaper in Britain (although *The Sun* actually has a smaller circulation than the *Mirror* these days, contrary to popular myth), but the idea that the right has control of the media goes beyond sheer numbers: right-of-centre newspapers in the UK tend to be very disciplined in their reporting, particularly around general election time, when there tends to be a circling of the wagons to protect the Conservative Party. The left-of-centre press, on the other hand, is generally far more diffuse and given to whims – the 2010 backing of the Lib Dems by *The Guardian* being a perfect example of a stance it is hard to imagine being replicated by a right-leaning outlet. Thus, there is a widespread feeling amongst the left that most media outlets, including ones like *The Independent*, *The Guardian* and the *Mirror* that are supposed to be on their side, are in fact stacked against them in what amounts to a conspiracy to keep anyone really radical from ever getting into No. 10. And by conspiracy, I mean a full-blown faked moon landing type of a thing. The popularity of hard-left outlets that have appeared over the past few years, the best example of which is the aforementioned Canary, all feed off the idea that this conspiracy is embedded in our mainstream media; an immutable part of how the press in this country functions as a whole.

Much recent ire on the left surrounds the right-leaning press outlets' continual attacks on Corbyn throughout the 2017 general election campaign regarding his attitudes towards the IRA. This, in a sense, is classic left-wing media bashing, one which misunderstands how political communications work, even on the most basic level imaginable. Corbyn could have killed the IRA story pretty much dead whenever he wanted to during the campaign. He simply had to say, 'I condemn the IRA and all those who commit acts of murder, for any reason, unreservedly' and it would have been hard for the press to continue attacking him on that front, however much there was a desire to from certain quarters. Given the peace that has existed in Northern Ireland since the 1998 Good Friday Agreement, it would have cost him nothing to have said this, either. For instance, it is possible to be in favour of a united Ireland and still disavow the IRA and its methods. To take a relevant modern analogy, one can be a passionate Scottish nationalist and still believe that any terrorism meant to bring about Scottish independence would not only be a terrible idea but one that would in the long run hurt the very cause it is supposed to be furthering (as one could credibly argue happened in Ireland with the IRA). No one was asking Corbyn to roll back on anything he believed in; they just wanted to know whether he thought terrorists who had committed atrocities on British soil were wrong to have done so or if there were times when he would accept that things in Britain needed to be destroyed by hostile groups, at least when British policy was deemed to have been incorrect.

The reason the press pursued the IRA question so vigorously was because it was relevant to Corbyn's character, and furthermore how he would go about protecting the country from hostile forces (which was very front and centre given the spate of terrorist attacks the country was suffering at the time). Would he protect British citizens and property no matter what – or would there be circumstances under which he would sympathise, at least to some extent, with the aggressors? It isn't a surprise that the press wanted an answer on that, and Corbyn continually refused to give it in a clear-cut way.

Of course, the truly ironic thing is that in the end, the right-of-centre press droning on and on about Corbyn's past dealings with the IRA probably helped Labour a little, not the Tories. They kept trying to paint him as someone dangerous, when all anyone saw was an avuncular old leftie. If the MSM of the left's imaginings were actually as powerful as they have always claimed, then the Tories should have romped home in the last election with the massive majority the very MSM predicted. The truth about the power of the right-wing media is a world away from the left's depiction of it these days. Their constant droning on about the MSM would be one thing against a backdrop of an incredibly powerful media that had vast resources. However, the reality is much more prosaic: newspapers in Britain are actually struggling, most of them downsizing in order to remain afloat, with even the biggest titles having difficulty funding investigative journalism. The myth of the big newspapers deciding elections in the UK is just that, as 2017 has surely demonstrated.

Instead of fighting the free press, liberals need to be strongly on the side of a completely free and open press. We face a period when political populism is on the rise at the same time as traditional news outlets are facing a squeeze. Having reporters who want to hold both the government of the day and the official opposition accountable isn't a luxury we can take or leave; it is one of the fundamental bedrocks of liberal democracy.

Putting aside the moral impetus behind the freedom of the press, just for the moment, there is actually a more practical concern at stake here as well. Instead of complaining that the press is doing them over and constantly trying to regulate the industry, progressives might do better to try work with the press as much as possible and make sure a liberal point of view is put forward more often. It is certainly worth a shot, seeing as how going on the offensive against the media hasn't worked all that well for the left.

Freedom of the press is something that exists in Britain because of the struggle towards it by progressives and progressive forces. What a shame that we now rely almost entirely on conservatives to uphold it.

CHAPTER 14

THE DANGERS OF POLITICAL CORRECTNESS AND IDENTITY POLITICS

About five years ago, a trope within politically correct identity politics on the left arose in certain media outlets, first in the United States but then travelling to Europe via the internet. It was centred on the practice of yoga, with the idea being that white people doing yoga were engaged in 'cultural appropriation', even going so far as to suggest that what was happening when they practised the ancient art was akin to imperialism or even outright racism. 'If you're white, there's not necessarily anything wrong with you doing yoga,' was an actual passage in just such an article talking about this meme.* The war against white yoga is representative of a body of ideas that are now being floated by the left that are very, very dangerous to the very future of progressive politics, both in Britain and elsewhere.

Political correctness started with good intentions. The original goal, when one goes back to the roots of proper political correctness as we know it today, back in the late 1980s, was that casual racism and misogyny would come to seem unacceptable. As anyone who was around at that time can attest, racist jokes were flung about with a lot more abandon than kids today can imagine, and there was a current of sexism running through adult male conversation that political correctness has managed to palliate to an amazing degree. However, anyone reasonable can see that it is a very long jump from saying that it is not in any way acceptable to call a woman a derogatory and misogynistic epithet to her face in front of her work colleagues, to the suggestion that white people shouldn't be allowed to practise yoga. Over time, political correctness has to a substantial degree morphed into a dangerous and deluded parody of itself.

---

* Maisha Z. Johnson and Nisha Ahuja, '8 Signs Your Yoga Practice Is Culturally Appropriated – And Why It Matters', Everyday Feminism, 25 May 2016, accessed 7 August 2017 at http://everydayfeminism.com/2016/05/yoga-cultural-appropriation/

Its close cousin, identity politics, is even more danger-ous. For starters, it goes against everything progressive politics is supposed to stand for, namely the idea that it should not be your skin colour, gender, accent and reli-gion that determine what you get out of life, but rather who you are as a person and the decisions you make. Talking up the differences between people is poison to the idea of inclusivity, yet this is precisely what identi-ty politics as currently practised by the Western left is doing. When you spend your time emphasising what it is that supposedly separates people of different cultures and races, it isn't all that surprising that the divisions between these identities become greater and even all-encompassing as a result. That has consequences that are the very opposite of what the left intends.

The far right is very much into identity politics itself, just with a different desired outcome. Instead of talking up differences between people in order that we may re-spect every nuance of every culture, the far right wishes to use those differences to keep people of different cultures apart from each other to the greatest possible degree, both metaphorically and literally. The problem is, despite coming from opposite places to start with, the identity politics of the left and the far right end up in exactly the same place. Once you make racism OK again within a left-wing setting (which is what the 'white yoga' trope is in the end), even if the racism is directed against only white males, you are *still making racism OK again.* The major difference is that the far left tends to do this unconsciously while the right does it with intent.

And the negative effects of this are always bound to be felt by minority groups most of all, not the majoritarian white male targets who have the numbers and the power to withstand racist and sexist attacks made at them without it affecting their lives or livelihoods very much if at all. Saying 'If you're white, there's not *necessarily* anything wrong with you doing yoga,' is a much shorter hop to 'If you're an immigrant, there's not *necessarily* anything wrong with, say, living in a traditionally native British neighbourhood' than I think most people on the left believe it is.

If the sort of cultural appropriation rules that mean white people can't do yoga are applied evenly, then can't American people say that anyone using cars anywhere in the world is culturally misappropriating the automobile and that unless everyone stops doing so they are committing something akin to racism? Ridiculous, obviously, but that is where the logic of 'reverse identity politics' leads you. Take the bizarrely patronising view of Islam and Muslims the left often takes, one which fails to understand the basic differences between, say, Salafism and run-of-the-mill Sunni Islam, despite the left being the ones who crow the loudest when sections of the right lump all Muslims in together. There can be a tendency within the left to see all Muslims as victims, as a besieged minority grouping, something that turns most adherents of Islam in the West off, not surprisingly. Islamist extremists, on the other hand, find the left easy to plug into as there is a shared victim mentality which comes coupled with a desire to see Islamic terrorism as nothing more than the inevitable result of 'Western imperialism'. If jihadism is absolutely the fault of Western foreign policy, this is an easy point of agreement for Islamists and the Western left to cohere around, despite all of their other values being out of sync with one another. This is how you end up with empty slogans on protest signs like 'Islam is Feminism', and with it an infantilisation of the debate around topics like the unfair and abhorrent targeting of Muslims in the wake of terrorist attacks which appear to be inspired by jihadism, something which only helps the far right seemingly win more of the argument than should ever be possible. A good example of this came in the commentary immediately following the London Bridge attacks in early June 2017, when you had pundits from the right saying '1.6 billion Muslims are trying to murder the rest of the world', while portions of the left claimed the attacks were nothing more than the result of cuts to the police budget.

That there is still too much institutional racism in Britain is undoubtedly true. Genuine sexism and racism should be called out, regardless of how embedded in our culture it seems. But making a new rule that says eating certain kinds of foods or doing certain types of exercise is off-limits to some people simply because of their skin colour isn't just political correctness gone too far – it is very, very racist in and of itself. Identity politics are like kryptonite to liberalism – the two ideologies cannot be in the same room together. The whole point of the original idea of political correctness was to make society easier for minority groups to get along in, and to start to recognise for ourselves how much casual racism exists. Similarly, the impulse behind identity politics seems to come from an admirable understanding of imperialist behaviour of the past and a desire to avoid repeating those same mistakes. How horribly ironic it would be if the final destination for both of them was to make society more racist and difficult for minority groups themselves.

CHAPTER 15

MY BRIEF DEFENCE OF THE LONDON METROPOLITAN LIBERAL ELITE

'If you are a citizen of the world, you are a citizen of nowhere,' said Theresa May from the pulpit at the Conservative Party conference in 2016, her first as Prime Minister. I spend a lot of time listening to politicians and so it takes a lot for any particular quote to stick with me for any appreciable length of time, yet that one has. I found it deeply offensive, mostly because of the deep hypocrisy involved. I suppose I had always figured that if ever I heard the leader of a British political party muttering protectionist mumbo jumbo, it would be a Labour one. Had Yvette Cooper said the same thing, I would have just giggled and mostly forgotten about it. What got to me about Theresa May saying it while in the guise of Tory Prime Minister was that the right were playing games with politics to assumed political advantage, and they clearly weren't thinking about the consequences of it all.

Far from being in the disastrous state that many of its politicians claim these days, Britain is actually in pretty good nick. It remains the fifth largest economy in the world.* The idea that the country is falling to pieces is obviously and observably untrue. However, the UK is not without significant problems to overcome. Much like France, Britain has one city that is much more prosperous than the rest of the country and, beyond even that, has great disparity in terms of regional inequality. No one can figure out how to rebuild reasonable economies in the seaside towns of England, for instance, and no policies have been advanced by any government to even begin to help this process along for decades. There remain places in the north of England and the Midlands in which heavy industry shut down decades ago and has been replaced by little else since, or at least not enough in terms of economic activity. Add to this the fact that the Union which makes the country literally what it is in the first place has become imperilled in the past few years, particularly with Scottish politics becoming an entity

---

* World Economic Forum: https://www.weforum.org/agenda/2017/03/worlds-biggest-economies-in-2017/

unto itself, added to the fact that the country is going to have to dislodge itself from the European Union after spending the past half a century involved in that project in one way or another.

In the midst of all this, London – and, more specifically, London's dreaded metropolitan liberal elite – is often singled out for opprobrium. The people who qualify for this definition live in London (obviously), are relaxed about immigration, apparently eat a lot of houmous (and a lot of other 'non-British food' that doesn't qualify as acceptable under the old imperial rule book), have (supposedly) sophisticated tastes in art and music, are intellectual (or have intellectual pretensions at the very least) – I could go on, but you know the routine. You can smell a member of the metropolitan liberal elite a mile away.

There is no question that London has problems and that they translate into issues for the whole of England to deal with. Property is too expensive in the capital. To be fair, that's because nowhere else in the country can compete with it in economic scale (in terms of both size and diversity), so the market dictates that if you want to be in London you have to pay a premium. If there were more cities like London in England, house prices in the capital would be more reasonable and, more to the point, if you wanted to be in a major city that had jobs in a field that interested you, then being in London would no longer be an absolute requirement, since by definition there would be other cities that you could choose from. This therefore leads me to think that you have to make the other major cities in England more attractive, not make London less so.

If London was filled with all of these left-leaning, immigrant-loving vegetarians who looked down on the rest of the country, all while being a net user of resources – in other words, if London was poorer than most of the rest of the country, a bit like Rome in relation to the rest of Italy – I would fully empathise with more of the outrage. Yet it is London that is the success story here; it is London, whether anyone likes it or not, that funds the rest of England, by and large, not the other way round. Whatever London is doing, it's working. The idea that London needs to change so that it becomes more like Clacton-on-Sea just doesn't bear any resemblance to reality. We need some way of getting some London-style success up to the north and the Midlands to spread the wealth of this country around a little bit, not fret about how many Middle Eastern delicacies Londoners are consuming.

Here's the thing: I was certainly not born into the MLE myself. I know very much about what it is like to live outside of London. And let me tell you this: it is so much better being in London, I can't even begin to tell you. Another thing: because of the liberal nature of the city, you certainly don't have to be from London to thrive here. That's why there's so many immigrants, remember?

Every other city in England needs to try to become more like London, not continually demonise the place as beyond the pale. If Liverpool, Manchester, Birmingham – I could go on here but you get the point – were more like London, that would be better for the country, wouldn't it? More foreign investment would be attracted to cities in England that aren't London, meaning that those places would have more money and more jobs, and the people who lived there would have more money and more jobs. Life could improve more and more for people living in those cities as more and more jobs followed this influx of investment. London is the model for this kind of success, so the blueprint already exists. Weirdly, I would expect Tories to understand this more than anyone else, given that it is market forces that make this so.

I couldn't call myself a progressive if I didn't firmly believe that a free, liberal, multi-racial society is better than a closed-off, immigrant-fearing one that looks to the past as a realistic model. In order to face the challenges of the twenty-first century, particularly with Brexit in the mix, Britain needs to be as forward-looking as possible.

Sure, the MLE can be pretentious and bit self-satisfied at times, but a society that rewards open-mindedness is a good thing, not a negative.

Particularly since the vote to leave the EU in June 2016, liberals have become over-apologetic. They want to seem like they 'get' the rest of the country, like they understand why the people of the north-east, say, wanted something different than what voters in London wanted. This shows the inherent decency of most liberals, but it has become tiresome: be proud to be liberal – it's a good thing. It is time to be proud to be a member of the metropolitan liberal elite again, I say, with the emphasis now on how we spread the wealth to the rest of the country, not on how to drag affluent parts of it down.

PART IV

LOOKING ABROAD FOR ANSWERS

CHAPTER 16

ON THE MOVE! LESSONS FROM FRANCE

Back when I had a job that took me to things like BALDE conferences, there were always plenty of jokes at France's expense around the bars of Brussels, built on the idea that La République has no liberals (the country has never had an electorally significant liberal party). As such, it was a welcome surprise to me that when it came time to write this book, the best place to look for a relevant recent example of centrism done well abroad happens to be France. Given the jokes about French liberals not so many years ago, I am led to believe that if it can happen in France then it really can happen anywhere, despite the British general election result making a genuine centrist alternative in the UK seem ever more distant.

Throughout the 35-odd years prior to the 2017

presidential election, the leadership of France swung between the Parti Socialiste and a couple of entities that came and went on the right, all of them representing a Gaullist political position, which, to very briefly explain, is much like classic Toryism in its seeking of consensus and pragmatism (supposedly, anyhow) over ideology. A fight that was witnessed on the right in Britain occurred in parallel in France, namely the battle between the Thatcherite economic neoliberals and the more traditional conservatives who see the state partly as a means to achieving a more homogenous society, to help faith, family and flag along on its way (in France, this battle even occurred within one man, in the form of Jacques Chirac). Neither side won that debate on the French right; the tension between the two camps was never really resolved, and right-of-centre French politicians always tried to walk the fence between them. Sarkozy, for instance, was the quintessential mixture of the two tribes, breaking with Napoleon's tradition of freeing prisoners on Bastille Day in a bid to seem tough on crime on one hand, while pursuing an Anglo-Saxon economic model, at least in spirit, on the other. One could argue the two sides destroyed each other, leading directly to Macron in some ways. Meanwhile on the left, the immense failure of François Hollande to effect change after running on a very left-wing, change-oriented platform (which he mostly chickened out of once he got to the Élysée) led to an approval rating of 4 per cent at one stage.*

Hollande's terrible poll ratings meant he wouldn't be running for re-election in 2017, and indeed that Parti Socialiste's chances of winning seemed remote whomever ran. The real break in the system came when the main challenger on the right, François Fillon, was caught up in a financial scandal. The chance to break open the two-party system appeared, but at first glance it was thought that it might lead to the election of Marine Le Pen, the leader of the far-right Front National. She had done much to detoxify the FN brand, and her mode of populism seemed to fit the French public mood of fear. But out of the blue rode the man of the moment, seemingly from nowhere (or at least, nowhere expected). Emmanuel Macron, a man running as the leader of a party that had existed for just over a year before the election that gave him the presidency, captured the hearts of the French nation. Or, at the very least, he did enough to seem better than Marine Le Pen. That's the thing about politics: sometimes luck counts for a lot, and who you get to run against is down to the whims of fate.

The history of Macron's party, En Marche! (rechristened La République En Marche! since the presidential

---

* Poll conducted for *Le Monde*, published 25 October 2016

election) is, as I said, miraculously brief given the level of power it has now obtained. At a meeting held on 6 April 2016 in Amiens, Emmanuel Macron's hometown, it was agreed to start a new movement amongst a small group of likeminded individuals. It was to be built on a form of centrism informed by the Third Way, but really was mostly launched around the figure of Emmanuel Macron himself (the initial initials of the movement/party corresponding intentionally to Macron's own personal acronym). Along the journey to the Élysée Palace, Macron defeated both of the two traditional parties of the right and left as well as a hard-right populist that many (myself included) thought would win. In an era defined by anti-EU, anti-immigrant sentiment, a pro-EU internationalist won 65 per cent of the vote. Of course, some credit for this must go to the way the French system itself operates (the traditional ganging up against the extremist in the presidential run-off doing for Marine Le Pen the same as it had done for her father more than a decade earlier), but it nonetheless remains an inspiration for British liberals. So, what did En Marche! do correctly that we haven't been doing on this side of the channel?

There are three reasons, beyond the vagaries of the system itself, that Macron won the presidency. The first is that he had something positive to say, offering hope along the way – and, more than that, his political personality suggested hope *combined with* competence, an important lesson for both the British left and UK centrists to understand. Positive change that can be delivered is what Macron seemed to stand for, and the French electorate responded by giving him not only the presidency, but also a parliamentary majority of some heft for his nascent organisation.

Two, by being happy to wear the right's clothes in certain policy areas, the economy most prevalently, he was able to undercut a lot of the would-be right-of-centre arguments about credibility and the ability to make tough choices (although a debate around the need for economic stability did not feature much in the British election of this year, directly to the right's detriment. May wanted to avoid talking about the economy in the same terms as Osborne, and lost the argument by default). Of course, some of these positions taken up by Macron offered him up to criticisms from the left, but this didn't significantly count against him.

Three, and most vital to what I will be talking about in the final part of this book, Macron started something new and therefore was not tied to the failings of past centre-left groupings. This is something often forgotten when discussing possible splits in the Labour Party: sometimes the past negative baggage a brand has can be equal to or greater than the positive aspects the brand summons forth in the minds of the electorate. The 2017 general election showed, as I have already stated, that the Labour brand does still have remarkable pull. However, it also seems stuck where it is; it has enough attraction for certain people to vote Labour no matter who is leader, yet it also repels other groups of voters who will be needed in order to win an election. Macron demonstrated that sometimes starting something new in politics is worth the associated risk.

All this begs the question: could a British Macron pull off the same feat? Although the differences in political systems are worth noting here, I do not believe the Westminster parliamentary system makes a new centrist party landslide impossible. Heroes have ridden to the rescue for progressive parties in the past (although they tend to be derided by the left for having done so in posterity – take, for instance, the one no one wishes to speak of these days, Tony Blair. He was the future once) and there is little reason to believe it wouldn't be possible again in the near future.

Inspired by Macron's victory, after the 2017 general election came and went, I decided to head to Paris to cheer myself up. I wanted to see the Macron parliamentary landslide happen at close quarters and witness the election that took place on 18 June to elect the new

French députées, which resulted in La République En Marche! taking 350 of 577 seats). I also wanted to talk to anyone connected to the new centrist French royalty, but rocking up in the 8th arrondissement and hoping for the best was not the most efficient way to go about this, as I soon discovered. Instead, I ended up mostly just soaking up the atmosphere and trying to dream of something similar taking place in London. Everyone I spoke to in my highly dodgy French, from the bars of the Left Bank to the coffee shops near La Bastille, told me they would be voting for La République En Marche! – no surprise, really, when you consider the current state of French politics, but mind-blowing when you stop and think about how badly the Lib Dems did in London in the general election just past (answer: very badly indeed).

'He gives us a hope we have not seen in a long time,' said one slightly sauced on wine denizen of a Montmartre establishment I always visit when I come to Paris. I asked her how she had voted in the previous presidential election.

'Hollande, of course!' she almost shrieked, looking slightly offended that I would have wondered how she could have possibly voted otherwise, despite the two of us having only met five minutes earlier. Yes, the lefties voted Macron. But so did much of the traditional French right, which was the real trick here.

'I was going to vote Fillon before that whole thing with his wife. But when I voted Macron in both rounds I had no doubts either time,' said Jean-Luc, a stockbroker in his mid-thirties originally from a small town in Massif Central, who spends his days toiling away in an office in La Défense but enjoys drinking in Montparnasse during the evening. I approached him in a small bar near Raspail after I heard him speaking English on his phone.

'New York,' he had said, pointing to the device. 'You can only get them around this time of day.'

He went on to tell me that he had voted for Sarkozy in 2012 and 2007, and for Chirac prior to that. I asked him if he thinks he'll stay with Macron next time, or if he'll move back to the UMP.

'This depends on two factors. One, how Macron performs as President. Remember, he could still be shit, we don't know. And two, if the UMP can survive En Marche! coming to power. This we don't know either. Macron could destroy the traditional right in this country.'

Will French politics become a straight fight between Macron's brand of centrism and Le Pen's form of hard-right populism from here on in, to the exclusion of the traditional left and right?

'Could be,' said Jean-Luc. 'Or next time out, it could be Parti Socialiste and UMP again as the main contenders. As you should know coming from Britain, making a prediction about what will happen to politics in the future, even the very near future, has become very, very unwise, no?'

Once Jean-Luc had had enough of me, I wandered out onto the Boulevard Raspail. I soon passed a young girl with an accordion, busking. She couldn't have been older than ten and yet she was all alone, singing a French version of 'Don't Dream It, Be It' from the *Rocky Horror Picture Show* soundtrack. I thought about throwing some money into her basket, but it felt wrong somehow, as if I were aiding and abetting child abuse. Where the hell were the people who were supposed to be looking after her? Instead, I stayed only a few more seconds before departing back up the road towards St-Germain, still feeling conflicted about whether I should have given the mini-busker some change.

The following day was the election, and as it became clear the landslide really was on for En Marche!, premature celebrations began to break out in the cafés of Paris. I watched it all with slight detachment, feeling glad it was happening yet sad that something similar was so epically distant from being possible in Britain. Perhaps centrism can be young, sexy and vibrant. But not in Britain – at least, not yet.

CHAPTER 17

WHAT CAN AMERICA AND BRITAIN TEACH EACH OTHER ABOUT THE FUTURE OF THE LEFT?

While there are many differences between the politics of the United States of America and those of Great Britain – the fact that the US has a presidential system with an elected upper house while Britain has a parliamentary system with an unelected upper house is just the tip of the iceberg – the malaise that has affected left-of-centre politics looks remarkably similar in both countries. Losing the economic competence argument to the right, despite the right having been less than fiscally sound; getting buried in identity politics and shedding more voters as a result; fighting a battle between the moderate centre left and the hard left that allows the right to come through the middle; suffering a severe lack of leaders who can appeal both to the base and to the wider electorate. Put this way, the tales of left-wing politics on either side of the Atlantic sound eerily similar.

It is in the differences between them that we begin to really understand the stories of the left in America and the left in the UK over the past decade. There have been plenty of comparisons made between Jeremy Corbyn and Bernie Sanders, for instance, many implying that the two are almost synonymous; perfect political cousins. While both self-describe as socialists while rolling out platforms that are wholly socially democratic instead (although in Corbyn's case, one senses this is down to gradualism born of pragmatism as opposed to anything more heartfelt), Sanders has many talents and qualities utterly lacking in Corbyn. For one, Sanders is a truly great public speaker (it is impossible to imagine him reading the line 'strong message here' off an autocue, for instance) while Corbyn is merely a mediocre one. Sanders is also from a working-class background and sounds and feels like a working-class politician, thus his ability to really speak to the white working classes in key swing states such as Pennsylvania and Ohio contrasts starkly with Corbyn's middle-class Islingtonian leftism.

As a result, Sanders's anger with the status quo seems genuine rather than affected, as it does with Corbyn.

Sanders is also working within a political culture that is considerably to the right of the one Corbyn inhabits in the United Kingdom, which has its upsides and downsides for Bernie. There is so much more social democracy that is visibly necessary in America, so a good communicator like Sanders can illustrate the great need for a leftist government, which would be harder to do in a Britain that already has a national health service, no matter how talented the espouser. The flipside of this is that his mostly modest proposals (apart from the eye-wateringly high rate of tax he speaks of now and again) sound a great deal more radical than the same policies would feel in Britain.

Moving directly onto the elephant in the room here: the thing I found most surprising about Trump's rise to the White House is that for years I had become convinced that when a psychopath who had no real idea what he was doing finally became President, he would be a Democrat (and I am intentionally using the masculine pronoun here for a reason). I figured that there was every possibility that someone from the hard left, probably from the ranks of the Occupy movement, would rise quickly through the DNC to become the Democratic presidential candidate as a result of the hard left having managed to take over the apparatus of that party. This leftist would then do a lot of things that America desperately needs to see happen – just for starters, introducing a single-payer healthcare system; comprehensively overhauling the tax system to make it easier to understand and less easy to find loopholes in; rolling out major transportation infrastructure; making vast improvements to the state education system so that not getting private schooling would no longer be the equivalent of having your life ruined by the age of seven. This would all have been done, in my vision of this psycho Democrat future, by creating a massive, completely unsustainable amount of debt, with the result being the President who had overseen the whole thing being impeached and replaced by a deficit hawk and/or the Democrats getting voted out at the next election. Either way, the Republicans would then have got in on a ticket of sorting out the mess made by the left, wondering whether to accept a lot of the changes made to the country as part of the deal (it is a lot harder to take away benefits once they've actually been received by the public, as the real Republicans are finding out now) or just to cut across the board. They would also have had to get over things like never raising taxes, as balancing the books after the previous President's profligacy would be obviously impossible without rises in taxation. The Republicans would become more like a standard centre-right party in Europe, taking on board a more classical liberal outlook.

I never thought the Republicans would ever nominate someone like Trump for lots of obvious reasons: no political experience, a complete lack of religious credibility, not to mention the fact that he was bound to say something unforgivably stupid along the way that would surely end his chances. I could never have foreseen that not only would the Republicans indeed nominate him, but they would do so with him having said more stupid things than anyone could ever keep up with, all while advocating protectionist economics and a massive shift in foreign policy outlook, items I would have thought would have killed him with the RNC for certain. To be fair, the Republican grandees really did try to kill off his run for a good while, and only accepted him as the nominee begrudgingly once it became obvious that it was an inevitability.

It seems that what did it for Trump was the anger that had grown into something truly dangerous in regards to political correctness and identity politics in America. This is similar to what has happened in Britain in some ways; it was almost certainly what fuelled the rise of UKIP, the notion that there were certain things that people were just not allowed to talk about, even though they may have been perceived as massive, unavoidable problems by certain segments of the population. I believe this factor was certainly helpful in leading to Brexit.

To find out if the comparisons between the American and British left were of any value, I found myself on my way to Washington, still reeling from my last sordid visit to America's capital, which had involved being quasi-kidnapped and taken to Rhode Island. On arrival, I stayed with my friend Blair, the very vision of obnoxious upper-middle-class Eastern Seaboard, Mid-Atlantic snobbery.

'Oh, Tyrone, couldn't keep away from our shores. Back for more fun, are we?'

'This time I'm trying to figure out what lessons there are for the British left in what happened with Bernie Sanders and then Trump.'

'Why are you still worrying yourself about the state of the British left?'

'I suppose I'm addicted to the subject.'

'Aren't you a Tory yet?'

'Not yet. So, can you help me?'

Blair suggested I get out of Washington immediately and see the flyover states for answers. I was mad enough to think he was onto something, so I rented a car and headed west, no fixed destination in mind. By the time I got to Ohio, I severely regretted my decision. Here's a quick review of Ohio for those of you unfamiliar with the Buckeye State: Toledo – sucks; Columbus – sucks; Akron – sucks; Cleveland – sucks; Cincinnati – you get the picture. In fact, it's hard to think of a time when I missed London more than when I was sat in a Subway just outside of Canton, watching a man who must have been at least thirty stone devour three foot-long sandwiches in the space of about ninety seconds, sweating profusely as he did so. Since he had held my attention for that whole period of time, I figured I could do worse than ask him about Bernie Sanders.

'The Jewish old guy, right?'

I nodded in the affirmative.

'Didn't he want to raise everyone's taxes?'

I nodded in the affirmative again.

'I liked him. I might have voted Democrat if he'd been the nominee.'

'Really?'

He thought again, briefly.

'Nah, I probably still would have voted for Trump.'

He then got up to walk to the counter. As I departed the restaurant, he sat down in the same booth (I had held it for him) to eat three more foot-long sandwiches he'd freshly ordered for himself, again doing so inside of two minutes while perspiring by the bucket load. I felt relieved I had managed to move away from his mouth.

I decided I had to get the hell out of Ohio and fast, and my overwhelming desire was to head to Chicago and hang out with my friends there, but then I realised that spending time with the American metropolitan liberal elite was not why I had come all this way. I forced myself to head to Michigan instead.

As I drove the interminable distance, I recalled in September 2016 discussing with a Republican strategist the chances of Trump taking Michigan in the election.

'Less likely than me living on the moon in a year's time, so stop thinking about it as a genuine possibility,' he had told me. Given that Trump carried the state by a mere 10,704 votes that November, I figured that the Great Lake State might have something to tell me about where the American left finds itself these days.

I eventually arrived in Ypsilanti, a very interesting little place. On one hand, it's a university town that was home to some of the yuppie culture that bled from nearby Ann Arbor in the 1960s. On the other, it was a major centre of automotive manufacturing once upon a time, back when those sorts of jobs still existed in America, and the part of the community that used to rely on that type of work has fallen on very hard times. It is thus an interesting cross-section of the urban metropolitan elite and the old working class. Speaking to the college kids just produced the usual stale crap you'd expect (anti-Hillary stuff based on unconscious or fully conscious sexism; Bernie is great, but they can't really say why that is), but one particular ex-factory hand gave me some perspective.

'I voted for Trump because I thought he was an asshole who gets things done. Turns out he's just an asshole.'

I'll end this chapter by trying to answer the following question: could a Trump-like character become Prime Minister of Great Britain? There is a temptation to compare Corbyn to Trump (men who rose to political prominence despite being outsiders within their own respective parties), but the attempt at similitude is ultimately false. The answer is: I don't believe someone like Trump could get into No. 10. Why? All I have to fall back on is a belief in British suspicion of demagoguery, even in a diluted form. Theresa May ran the 2017 general election on the basis of seeking a large majority in order to have a free hand in the Brexit negotiations; the British public wasn't in the mood to hand such a thing over. I don't think they would be minded to do something like it again in future, cither.

CHAPTER 18

ROLLING WITH CIUDADANOS

The coach trip alone was enough to make me think that perhaps I'd made an egregious error. Twenty-four hours all told (which includes the Channel ferry, to be fair), so by the time we got to the Franco-Spanish border I was ready to have a nervous breakdown. Then came one of those perfect-timing jobs: the sun started to rise just as we crossed the international boundary, and I swear, the moment we were in Spain everything began to look, well, incredibly Spanish, not surprisingly enough, and with that I finally settled into the idea that this trip to Barcelona to find out what I could about Ciudadanos, a relatively new centrist party, was worth all the hassle. My heart swelled a little as I looked down on the red rooftops atop the Catalan villas; that sudden feeling that rural Spain always gives me of being inside of a spaghetti western and loving every second of it.

A brief word about Ciudadanos: they were founded in 2006 as a Catalonian party dedicated to the province remaining part of Spain (in opposition to the sizeable Catalan independence movement). They declare themselves as centrist in ideological philosophy, and this centrism has helped to find them an audience outside of Catalonia. They have only ever had one leader, the charismatic Albert Rivera, a man who once appeared in the buff on a campaign poster to help garner interest in the party (it worked). I'm interested in Ciudadanos for the same reasons La République En Marche! appeal to me: I want to understand what the ingredients are for a successful liberal, centrist party, and since we don't have anything like that in Britain at present, one must look abroad.

'Hey, let me ask you something,' I said to my Chicago connection as I left a shop just outside of Barcelona with my *agua* in hand. 'Is "Hola" like the French "voila"?'

My American chum then did what both of us do when the other has said something notably stupid: a blank, dead expression accompanied by a hanging out of the jaw meant to indicate shock of a brain-scrambling nature.

'You're going to Barcelona to interview some Spanish political types and your ability to speak Spanish doesn't extend to knowing how to say hello?'

'Most of them speak English. And anyway, that's why you're here, remember?'

My Chicago connection had his high school-level Spanish to fall back on, which was ostensibly his reason for tagging along. Once we arrived in Barca, we met a lot of people quite quickly, many of whom we formed relationships with that managed to last no more than a few days, all of them under the pretence of finding someone connected with Ciudadanos to chat with but never coming close to achieving this objective. Probably the most successful of these transient friendships was with a vendor who called himself Ronaldo, an Andalusian guy in his mid-twenties who was selling dodgy tourist tat on the side streets of the Barri Gotic, or Las Ramblas itself on days when he felt particularly bold (it is a lot harder to run from the cops on the main drag). His English wasn't great but we weren't being picky; he would tell us about his childhood growing up in a *blanco* (white village); how it was beautiful and how he missed Andalucía so much but it was simply too hard to make a living there, even in the bigger cities like Málaga or Seville. He liked football a lot, as his nickname would have led you to believe. This greatly annoyed my Chicago connection, who had that in-built American aversion to the sport, so Ronaldo and I tended to talk about it only when he wasn't around, which wasn't very often. He said he knew some people who worked for Ciudadanos (how this was so was never made clear, but I took him at his word) and that he would arrange an interview for me. At the time, he was the only vague connection to the party I had located.

Within a week, we'd got in the habit of waking up in the *pensión*, getting a cheap breakfast somewhere, then walking down to La Barceloneta to meet with some ropey peripatetic acquaintances before hanging out on the beach, then walking back to the Barri Gotic in the afternoon to meet up with Ronaldo to catch happy hour in one of the bars we often frequented, a time when the drinks were even cheaper than usual, only to crash out in the *pensión* when we'd had enough, ready to get up and do it all over again come the morning. But still no Ciudadanos. My attempts to go in through the front door of the party brought me no joy either, one particularly embarrassing episode taking place at the party HQ in which my lack of Spanish was keenly felt.

And then, out of the blue, I caught a break. Someone who works for Ciudadanos, ferrying not only between Barcelona and Madrid but also to Brussels, called me out of the blue to say that if I was still interested in knowing about the party, I should meet him at a particular bar that was thankfully already very familiar to me in the Barri Gotic that evening at 8 p.m. His name was Eduardo (it wasn't really, but that's what we're going to call him) and he was tall, good-looking and terrifyingly young. His English was excellent, vindicating my decision to leave my Chicago connection back at the *pensión*.

'To understand the story of Ciudadanos fully, we need to start with the end of the dictatorship in 1975,' Eduardo kicked off with, assuring me that although he was fresh-faced, he was going to give me the real lowdown.

From the death of Franco to the signing of the constitution, Spain experienced three years of horrific violence. The communists would storm wealthy neighbourhoods and do what amounted to sacking them; the fascists, who still had a lot of the state apparatus on their side including most of the military, would enact mass killings of people with supposed communist sympathies. When the constitution was signed and what emerged was a two-party system, people welcomed it as a relief from the violence.

The two-party system was a fix, really. The parties knew that they would need to trade power now and again, but the same system of cronyism, nepotism, corruption, all that continued regardless of whether it was the socialists or the Christian Democrats in government. No one side wanted to call the other out on any of their worst habits, since they wanted to do the same things next time they got into power themselves.

But the dictatorship was a long time ago now, and everyone other than the oldest generation either has few memories of it or was not even born at the time. Pressure began to be applied by the electorate upon the two main parties to change their ways about a decade ago, but they were sure the gravy train could continue on and on and on. And so, this created political space: both on the left with Podemos, and in the centre with Ciudadanos.

Ciudadanos started in Barcelona as a regional Catalonian party, dedicated mostly to stopping the Catalonian independence movement. But it seems like the political message of Ciudadanos, which was free market but socially liberal, pro-European, all these centrist-type things, had an audience all over Spain. And so, in the last few years, Ciudadanos has expanded across the whole country and has become the fourth party of Spain, behind the two traditional parties and Podemos.

I asked Eduardo what the rise of Ciudadanos has to teach British centrists who pine for something similar in the UK.

'We knew who our target audience was and we went after their votes – and *only* their votes – single-mindedly.'

And your target audience was?

'Young internationalists, often self-employed, particularly in sectors like tech. University students, the business community. We avoided older people and public-sector workers.'

How did you target these groups?

Social media was key. But so was the message, which was anti-corruption on one hand but also optimism. We always keep things positive, since too much negativity turns our core audience off. The right can complain about the country going to hell because of receding values, and the left can moan about the country going to hell because of lack of public investment in services, but the centre, to win, must be relentlessly positive.

What else?

Leadership is so key. When I look at the UK, I wonder where your shining knight is. With Ciudadanos, we have always had Albert; in France, the En Marche! thing would never have happened without someone like Macron at the head of it. I don't know, maybe there is someone in British politics who is up and coming, someone I wouldn't know about, that might be such a figure?

I shook my head. He frowned.

'Then this will make things very difficult for you!'

At this point, Eduardo said that he had to get going shortly, so I asked him about his impression of the Lib Dems. He wrinkled his face up.

> I would like to say more nice things about them, you know. But being honest, I see a lot of problems there. Although I hate to say it as a passionate pro-European, I think they got it all wrong on Brexit somehow. It seems like the audience they were trying to get with that second referendum didn't listen at all. I have covered this already, I know, but leadership, this is a huge problem for the Lib Dems. The party also doesn't seem to be reaching the sort of audience we're reaching, the young, tech-savvy, urban types. I don't see how a centrist party can win anywhere without that group of people being firmly on side.

I thanked Eduardo and told him I would take care of the drinks as he dashed out the door. The sun was going down, and although I could have wandered around town on my lonesome, I decided to head back to the *pensión* instead.

'Get what you need?' my Chicago connection asked me as I entered the room. I nodded.

'You filled with bright ideas about how to save the centre of British politics, then?' he asked sarcastically.

'No. I probably know a lot more about what to avoid doing if that's the goal, but nah, I still don't know how to fix the centre of British politics.'

'At least we got to hang out with Ronaldo.'

'At least we got to hang out with Ronaldo, yes. And any excuse to come to Barcelona is probably a good one, whatever it might be.'

We decided to spend our last night in Spain bar hopping and having fun. After a few jars of Estrella, I found myself thinking that there probably will be some way to revive British centrism, somehow, some day; it will just suddenly open up for us. I believe it was almost certainly the beer doing the thinking at that point.

CHAPTER 19

OTTAWA AND THE FICTITIOUS CULT OF TRUDEAU

Time for a confession: despite having lived the vast majority of my adult life in England, and having always been through my parents a British citizen, I grew up in Canada. It wasn't an experience I look back on with fondness for many reasons, but let's leave that story for another time (it partly involves psychopathic ex-nuns and people of Scottish origin). Suffice it to say, I tend to avoid Canada and indeed Canadians as well, as usually any contact between those from the Great White North and myself ends in conflict in one sense or another. Thus, trying to figure out what was behind the rise of Justin Trudeau was something I avoided for a good long while.

The truth was, his election oddly irked me. For a period of time, my alienation from the land of my boyhood fitted in very nicely with my political beliefs. While that right-wing, theocratic weirdo Stephen Harper was in charge, I could very happily dispel people's assumptions about Canada being some sort of liberal wonderland as being incongruous with the basic facts. With Canada suddenly embracing a young, charismatic, liberal (and Liberal) Prime Minister at the same time as Europe was about to slide into populist right-wingery, I suddenly had this cover rather cruelly ripped away from me. Canada was hip again, and I would have to roll with it.

For those of you unaware, Ottawa, the capital of Canada, is considered a hellhole even by Canadians happily predisposed towards their own country. Phony feeling, oddly parochial and bizarrely undefined, Ottawa is best avoided. Think of it as Islamabad in the snow. I arrive there to examine the new Trudeau era in wintertime, a terrible move on my part. For those of you who have never experienced a Canadian winter, take a ten-minute stroll in a walk-in freezer in a T-shirt and shorts and then bear in mind that this is what Canada feels like on a warmer than usual day in December. Christ, my birthday is in December too – what was I thinking?

I fly over on Air Canada (called Air Communist by

Canadians for its poor standard of in-flight service), a nine-hour ride through purgatory only made bearable by the European lager I have brought with me onto the flight. (A common myth in Europe is that Canadian beer is preferable to American lager. It isn't, they are both equally terrible, but at least America has some beers that are acceptable, while all of the main Canadian brands are obnoxiously awful.) The in-flight film almost kills me, however: *Goin' Down the Road*, a 1970 film about two feckless men from Nova Scotia who come to Toronto ostensibly to find work but then actually spend all of their time drinking, hitting on women and saying things like 'What's life all aboot?' to each other. Canada's media, and by this I mean all films, TV, music, news, novels, magazines, you name it, all fall under what are known as the CANCON rules, or 'Canadian content'. Literally everything that is exposed to Canadians has to be judged sufficiently Canadian in order to pass muster. This has all sorts of horrific outcomes. My early twenties were blotted by scores of Canadian bands that would make soundalike Nirvana or Smashing Pumpkins songs, getting them on the radio only because they qualified under CANCON.

We finally land. Once I've got my luggage off the carousel, it's time to face the music. That horrible Arctic wind hits me hard the second I leave the sanctuary of the terminal building. At least Canada has decent public transport, so I'm soon in the centre of things – at least as 'centre of things' as it gets in Ottawa.

I try wandering around outside the governmental buildings for a while to get a sense of the place, but it's too bloody cold and I'm soon ensconced inside a Tim Hortons, supping a very mediocre cup of tea (seriously, why is it that in 2017 you can only get a decent cuppa in Britain? Surely it isn't that complicated). The place is crawling with lobbyists due to its location and I have to smile: lobbying is pretty much the same everywhere you go. The same careful conversations between public affairs people and MPs, always staying on *just* this side of the line; the same phone discussions had by the public affairs folks back to home base after the MP and his researcher have departed, always toning down expectations appropriately (he didn't say he would give a speech in the House *exactly*...); the same shop talk after the meeting, during which the lobbyists spend time complaining about the supposed uselessness of the political party with which they are most closely affiliated.

My first meeting of the day is with a few NDP representatives. The NDP are the hard-left party in Canada; sort of like Labour if they'd always remained small and weird. The NDP had their breakout moment at the 2011 general election, when they gained sixty-seven seats, mostly off the nationalist Bloc Québécois, to become the official opposition to Harper's Tories. Unfortunately for them, the NDP wave seemed to be mostly based on the popularity of their then leader, Jack Layton, who died only three and a half months into the subsequent parliament. Come 2015, the NDP were reduced to their more familiar third-party status, losing fifty-one seats as the Trudeau tsunami hauled in most left-of-centre votes.

Three older men walk into the room I've been placed in, after having received another not so great cup of tea to keep me company in the interim. They resemble a 'three stages in the life of Jeremy Corbyn' exhibition, with the youngest having a beard and slightly longer, very 1970s hair; the middle one is greying around the temples with a salt and pepper beard flowing out beyond them; the oldest of the three looks like Jeremy's doppelgänger.

'Anyone get you a doughnut, eh?' the middle-aged Corbyn clone asks me, and I am forced to answer in the negative. We move on from sugar-based snacks and onto politics.

'What's the future of the NDP?' I ask as a broad question to get the ball rolling. Silence from the other side of the table. The three men all look sideways at each other, as if I'd asked them about a criminal case they were all involved in at present, as opposed to throwing them the world's slowest of slow balls.

'I don't know really know, eh,' the eldest finally takes it upon himself to answer. 'Why did you have to start with such a hard one, eh?'

The other two laugh in recognition. While I wrack my brains for a softer question and can only come up with 'Why are men with beards so attractive to potential sexual partners?' the youngest one pipes up.

'I was going to ask you a question, eh: why did Jeremy Corbyn lose that election? He was totally going to win, eh.'

'What gave you the impression Jeremy Corbyn was ever going to win that election?' I ask him in return.

'That's what we were told, eh,' says the middle one with a shrug.

'By whom exactly?' I ask.

'The party,' says the older one who looks exactly like Jeremy Corbyn.

'I don't understand,' I say. 'The NDP sent you a briefing saying "Jeremy Corbyn will definitely win the general election"? When?'

'We got it about a week before your general election, eh,' the youngest one says cheerfully. None of them seem to understand how weird I think the whole thing is or why.

'More important question: who do you think will win the Cup this year?' the middle guy then asks, I think as a way of defusing the tension that has now arisen between myself and the NDP trio.

'Which Cup?' I ask in earnest. The three of them laugh heartily, simultaneously, sure I must be joking.

'We think the Senators have a real shot this year, but Jim here thinks the Canadiens will take it, eh,' says the older one. I realise as he points down the table that I have no idea which of the other two is Jim, as none of them actually told me what their names are. At least this comment, while leaving me in the dark about who Jim is, tells me what they are referring to with the 'Cup' – ice hockey, what else. Unfortunately for the three beards, I know nothing about ice hockey, don't follow it, don't like the sport even slightly. This, you are probably not aware, is not acceptable behaviour for any Canadian to engage in, so I try to close this line of enquiry down swiftly and quietly.

'Yeah, I think it'll be the Canucks' year.'

They all go silent after I say this and trade very concerned looks. I have said something really wrong, apparently. The Canucks are Vancouver's team, and I figure perhaps they are about to express some west coast dislike.

'The Canucks are bottom of the league,' says the youngest NDPer in an almost litigious fashion, 'so how are they going to win the Cup exactly, eh? They won't even make the playoffs!'

I have no choice but to come clean at this point.

'Look, guys, I've lived in England for around twenty years now, so I'm not really up on who's doing well or not in the NHL these days.'

The rest of the meeting from there is a bit of a blur; I recall a lot of shouting and pointing. I manage to get out of the building alive, that's the main thing.

For my next meeting, I have to go to the suburbs to meet someone at a shopping mall. Hazeldean, the place is called, and it turns out to be a nightmare to get to without a car. I find myself taking several buses and getting lost a few times along the way. Then, to add insult to injury, the guy is twenty minutes late.

'Hey, buddy,' he says as he arrives, and my heart sinks as I recall our sole phone conversation, one in which he said 'buddy' an awful lot. I give him space to apologise for being tardy – nothing doing. I mutter 'Canuck ****' under my breath and we then head to the mall's food court to see out the chat.

The guy's name is Gil McKeckhern, which, just for the record, is the most Canadian name it is technically possible to have. He's a journalist who apparently worked for the Liberal Party during the 2015 general election campaign in the communications department and had spent some time with Trudeau himself during this period.

'So, what gives, buddy?' he asks as we sit down. I'm

momentarily stunned as I forget how to speak Canadian, but then recover myself.

'Tell me as straightforwardly as you can: what's Justin Trudeau like?' I ask Gil.

'Well, buddy, he's harsh but fair. Firm but flexible. Kind but occasionally weird. Dizzy yet brilliant. Demanding yet doesn't give the slightest bullcrud, buddy.'

He pauses for a moment. I get the sense the aforementioned description of the Canadian Prime Minister is a party trick he pulls out of the bag all of the time, usually to great aplomb.

'You've never met him, have you?' I ask. Gil instantly crumbles, like a pie crust being hit with a hammer.

'He walked past me once, buddy. It was super sweet.'

'All right, moving past Trudeau, what was working for the Liberals like during the election?'

'It was brutal yet brilliant, buddy. Fast but slow as snail snot. Soul-destroying yet...'

'Oh Christ, you've never worked for the party either, have you?'

'I delivered some leaflets, buddy. It was freaking cold out there.'

'Jesus! I hauled myself all the way out to this shitty suburb for nothing?'

'Not for nothing, buddy: I've got some quality hooch in the trunk of my car. Wanna get wasted, buddy?'

I don't want to have to trudge back towards the heart of Canada's capital just yet, so I figure why not scoff some homemade liquor with Gil.

'Let her rip, buddy,' he says as he hands me the bottle after he has got into the driver's and I into the passenger's seats of his shitty '83 Chevy Impala.

'I'll tell you what, Gil,' I say, after taking my first swig. 'That was nowhere near as awful as I was expecting.'

'I often get that compliment, buddy.'

He turns on his car stereo, which begins to blare out some random section of Meatloaf's *Bat Out of Hell II* album.

'I see Canadian tastes in music are pretty much where they were the last time I was here,' I say.

'I can find you something snootier, buddy.'

'No, no, leave it on. I'm going for an authentic experience here.'

We get drunk pretty quickly, as you can well imagine. After the bottle is finished, Gil reaches behind him to grab something. I figure it must be another bottle of the homemade bootleg.

'Thanks, but I can't drink any…'

I stop short as my drinking companion is now pointing a revolver at me.

'Is that thing loaded, Gil?'

'It sure is, buddy.'

'Why, Gil?'

'Why not, buddy?'

I hear a click and then...

I'll stop that right there. By now you've worked out for yourself that I didn't go to Ottawa and meet three bearded Jeremy Corbyn lookalikes and then go to a mall where I met a Liberal charlatan who fed me illegal liquor before killing me with a pistol. This didn't happen because one, the budget of this book did not extend to such a journey, and two, because I didn't need to be physically in Canada to know why Justin Trudeau managed to become a Liberal Prime Minister when so many others before him had failed. It's the same thing that the elections of Macron and Sadiq Khan showed us. Liberals can win elections when they are led by someone charismatic and able; when they present a policy agenda that sounds plausible and hopeful and is relatively immune to attacks from the right; when it focuses on vision and pragmatism over left-wing purism. Saying it like that, it doesn't sound so difficult, does it?

Trudeau won in Canada because he looked and sounded the part, took the task dead seriously, and surrounded himself with competent people to achieve the task of winning, leaving the Gil McKecherns of this world out of it. Corbyn hasn't done any of those things. Sometimes politics really isn't all that hard to understand.

PART V

WHAT HAPPENS NEXT

CHAPTER 20

HOW THE FUTURE COULD BE LIBERAL SOCIAL DEMOCRACY — IF WE ALL WANT IT BADLY ENOUGH

Social democracy just isn't as sexy as Marxism. First of all, it tends to be about pragmatically solving bread-and-butter problems – how do you design systems that save the state money on public services without affecting those services at the coal face? How can you make prison sizes smaller without making crime increase? – as opposed to running around with a Kalashnikov while wearing a beret, thinking all the while that grand ideological structures solve everyone's problems automatically once they have been laid over a society. Having said that, what social democracy has as a merit that socialism does not is that it has a decent track record of having been successfully carried out, whereas everywhere that proper socialism has been attempted to date, as I elaborated on in Part II, it has been an unmitigated disaster.

This hasn't stopped the left from engaging in a sort of formless nostalgia for socialism in principle, all while clinging to social democracy in actual policy terms. The best recent example of this is the Labour 2017 general election manifesto itself. Look at the headline policies: scrap tuition fees, nationalise the water companies, railways, buses and Royal Mail, 45 per cent tax on any earnings over £80,000 a year, the reintroduction of the 50 per cent tax rate on those earning over £123,000 per annum, protect the triple lock on pensions and make zero-hours contracts illegal. It's unquestionably left-wing, yet it's hardly Marxist-Leninism, is it? For instance, where is the plan for nationalising everything: the supermarkets, the manufacturing sector, banks, the technology sector, infrastructure building?

The 2017 Labour manifesto exhibited a particularly leftist strain of social democracy, I'll give you that, but why bother with the Trotskyist posturing if what you really want to enact in power is soft-Milibandism? Yet whatever the policy detail advocated, Corbyn sees himself as a socialist and his followers see themselves as socialists, and there's the rub.

With that in mind, I offer this challenge to the left

here and now: outlaw the word 'socialism' if you want to really succeed electorally ever again – as in, win a general election, not think 262 seats is worth crying out of joy over. The term is not only politically toxic but, as I've already said, isn't even what anyone on the left, centre left, or liberal centre seriously wants to carry out anyhow. Get rid of it; socialism is a relic of the twentieth century, where it should stay.

This lack of clarity isn't mere semantics; it clouds the vision of what the left of centre actually wishes to achieve, the society it actually wants to foster, thus leading to the sort of situation you had in the general election campaign when Labour and the Lib Dems went on the offensive against the so-called dementia tax, despite the attack making no real sense from an ideological perspective. From a Tory viewpoint, the portion of the Conservative 2017 manifesto which stated that social care in the home provided by the state must be paid back out of the proceeds of the sale of the person's estate after death was anathema to everything traditionally Tory, both to the grey vote the party relies upon to turn out on polling day as well as to the free market portion of the Conservative fold. It could be plausibly argued that the 'dementia tax' was the most socialist policy in either of the two main parties' manifestos prior to the last general election. On top of the ideological issue, Labour attacked the policy in a way that made little sense: 'The Tories are planning to make people pay for care in their own home unless they have less than £100,000 in assets. This will leave thousands of the most vulnerable at risk of losing their homes and is something many are calling a "dementia tax".'*

Bear in mind that the Labour manifesto makes it clear that anyone who earns £80,000 a year should pay more in tax – so why then are people who have more than £100,000 in assets considered 'the most vulnerable'? The point I'm making is not that Labour shouldn't have tried to play politics with the Tories – that's what general election campaigns are mostly about – but that there was no thought at all given to consistency in the attack. Labour obviously got away with this, but you can't run from consistency for ever.

Also, 'dementia tax' as a slogan reminded me a lot of the 'bedroom tax' from a few years previous. Given that the left wants to promote the idea that higher taxation in order to fund public services is a good thing, do they not see that it is counterproductive to create a string of pejorative catchphrases for policies which all end with the word 'tax'? I realise they are playing on the negative associations involved in the word in question, but it does

---

* www.labour.co.uk/index.php/splash/Conservative-social-care-plans, accessed 9 August 2017

make it lot harder to then reclaim the term and save it for future positive use.

The left never seems to realise that the Conservative Party can get away with the ideological U-turns it often engages in because it is by definition a non-ideological vessel; the whole point of the party is to gain power and use it in a way that is deemed practical, without recourse to grandiose political philosophies getting in the way. This is, of course, nonsense in practice: the Conservative Party can be as ideological as any party when the mood strikes. One need only recall Margaret Thatcher slamming Hayek's *Road to Serfdom* down on the Cabinet table and declaring, 'This is what we believe in' for anecdotal evidence of that. However, the Tories are not beholden to any one particular ideological concept, whereas the left is supposedly all about advancing a specific mode of thought (although again, whether that's socialism or a sort of watery type of social democracy many a wet Tory could happily live with is another matter). When the left contradicts itself, in other words, *it matters*. That may seem a little unfair, but those are the rules.

In the meantime, it would have been very easy to construct a liberal critique of the 'dementia tax': one of the cornerstones of the British system is that people get free emergency healthcare at the point of service. We as liberals feel that this should apply equally to those who are elderly and cannot care for themselves, just as they should for anyone else. We also do not feel that people who have worked all of their lives to build assets should have them stripped away by the state simply because they have had the misfortune to fall too ill to continue caring for themselves.

Liberalism, for all its supposed slipperiness, is actually not all that hard to define. *Every person deserves to be given the best shot at the life they want to live.* That's it, really, all there is to it. I suppose I could add a second thought here: *The more happy and productive people there are in society, the more happy and productive the society is as a whole.* The aim of a liberal society is to move as many people as possible into the active economy and thus minimise inequality to a sustainable level. You can never eliminate inequality completely (none of the socialist experiments of the twentieth century came remotely close to achieving this goal), and in a sense, nor should that even be desirable. In order to live in a free society, one in which people can work when they like and not work if they don't wish to, you have to accept that some level of inequality is inevitable.

This is why the ideas espoused by the hard left, such as they are, don't strike the chord in certain people that its adherents think they should. *People like to own stuff.* I recall one particularly well-cited individual within the

British left (whom I will not name in order to save his blushes/avoid giving him free publicity) at an event a few years back announcing to the gathered, 'We need to create a society in which people buy less useless crap,' something that got a round of applause from the lefties in the crowd. And I thought, no, we don't need that; what we need is a society that isn't obsessed with useless crap simply because more than half the population will never be able to own some of it. This is, in a way, the strangest element of modern left-wing ideology: the whole thing seems to be based on sharing out stuff equally amongst everyone, and yet at the same time, stuff isn't supposed to matter in the slightest. Which is it then? If stuff doesn't matter, who cares if one guy owns twelve yachts while another owns nothing whatsoever? Why is poverty actually a bad thing so long as people can eat and have a roof over their heads?

I'll tell you why poverty is bad, as someone who has experienced rather extreme forms of it at different times in his life: when you are really poor, you have very few real choices. You hate your job? You have to trudge to it, otherwise you won't have enough to make the rent or buy food. Hate where you live? You're stuck there. What's really awful about being really poor is that your options are so narrow; it is the lack of choice in every single aspect of one's life that makes poverty the horror that it is.

While it may seem sometimes as if the deck is stacked against liberals, time is on our side: young people in Britain today are more socially and economically liberal than ever before.* Those aged 18–24 are socially liberal, as many would expect, taking a liberal view on equal marriage, non-traditional family structures, drug legalisation. But, contrary to the commonly held image of the millennial protesting with a T-shirt equating Jeremy Corbyn with either Jesus Christ or Che Guevara, they are also more economically liberal as well: young adults 'are more likely than older people to consider social problems the responsibility of individuals rather than government'.† Part of the lackadaisical attitude a lot of young people have towards social democracy is undoubtedly because they take it for granted. Having lived in a society with a high level of public services and a free at the point of use single-payer healthcare system, they cannot imagine things any other way.

Of course, there is another cohort of young people who are obviously in thrall to Corbyn, but again, looking at the policies from the last Labour manifesto, most of them are firmly socially democratic anyhow, and a lot

---

* 'Generation Boris', *The Economist*, 1 June 2013, accessed 10 August 2017 at: https://www.economist.com/news/britain/21578666-britains-youth-are-not-just-more-liberal-their-elders-they-are-also-more-liberal-any

† Ibid.

of what young Corbynistas seem to shout loudest about in terms of liking the Corbyn agenda is the socially liberal stuff: the support for minority rights, the pro-immigration outlook. It seems to me that we can find a middle ground where young liberals and young social democrats who may have taken a slight wrong turn with the Corbyn project can make common cause. There is a whole generation out there waiting to be brought together under one banner.

The Tories have started to embrace social democracy, even if it's only out of political expedience for the time being. They've also learned that if you're going to attempt to do it, you have to do it well, as Theresa May demonstrated in reverse – she talked a lot of rhetoric, but under-delivered in policy terms, which the public noticed. While many on the left may think that the Tories will never be believed as a party that can deliver social democracy, they shouldn't be so cavalier on that front either. No one thought Corbyn could do anything but lose seats, if you'll recall. The current era affords no complacency to anyone.

CHAPTER 21

COULD THE SDP MARK 2 EVER BE A REAL THING?

I had high hopes for the possibilities around an SDP Mark 2 at the start of the general election campaign, let's call it the 'Democratic Party' for now; a brand-new centrist, liberal party that would be dedicated to a socially liberal, social market agenda. As it turned out, the result of the election made this possibility look more remote than ever. For the time being at least, Labour MPs will almost certainly be terrified to leave the comfort of the party they are currently in, having seen first-hand how much value there is in the Labour brand. For instance, it is worth noting that Simon Danczuk, former Labour MP for Rochdale, ran as an independent candidate at the 2017 general election in the same constituency he had won with a 12,000 majority in 2015 as a Labour candidate. This time out, he finished fifth with 883 votes, while Tony Lloyd, the Labour candidate who replaced him, increased Labour's majority by just shy of 12 per cent. For all those Labour MPs out there who think they have a 'personal' vote, this was a strong rebuke.

The Lib Dems also stalled at the 2017 election, gaining some and losing other seats while their share of the vote continued to decrease, proving that their ability to be a sort of pre-vessel for this new party was sadly lacking. I would argue that the failure of the Liberal Democrats to improve substantially at the last general election was not a demonstration of the lack of appetite for a centrist party, but rather down to the faults, past and present, of that particular party. I believe there is still a desire out there for a centrist party, but one shorn of the baggage and idiosyncrasies of the Lib Dems. In fact, the case for a new centrist party is stronger than ever when you actually look at the current situation free from individual career aspirations or internal Tory and Labour party politics.

In 1981, the Labour Party was led by Michael Foot. He was actually, as many forget these days, the relatively centrist candidate, meant to bring together the warring left and right factions of the party into a united, stable force capable of winning an election. Unfortunately, the party continued to drift leftwards and four Labour MPs decided one day that they had had enough. Quickly becoming known as the Gang of Four, David Owen, Shirley Williams, Roy Jenkins and Bill Rodgers decided to announce that they were leaving the Labour Party and setting up a new outfit called the Social Democratic Party. They would get to 50 per cent in the opinion polls at one stage before receiving 25 per cent of the national vote share at the 1983 general election. However, that same election saw them ending up with fewer seats than they'd started with and they eventually merged with the old Liberal Party to become the modern Lib Dems we know and love a few years later. All told, the SDP experiment lasted a paltry seven years.

The SDP is mostly looked back on as a failure and furthermore as a warning to members of the two major parties that splits always supposedly lead somewhere negative. However, there were several sides to the SDP story that are not reflected upon enough by those who would write them off completely. For starters, the main problem the SDP had in gaining traction is that they weren't big enough to start with. In retrospect, they failed upon launch, the 50 per cent poll leads and the favourable press write-ups off the back of champagne buffets being simply red herrings. They had only twenty-eight members of the PLP defect to them when they started out, and only one Tory MP to boot. This was never going to be enough to overtake Labour as one of the two main players in British politics, which must surely have been the aim of the SDP in the minds of its progenitors. If over a hundred and fifty Labour MPs had left in September 2016 to start a breakaway party (or if they left now, for that matter), while it would have had no guarantee of success by any means, it would not have failed for the same reasons as the SDP did. Imagine if the launch of the SDP in 1981 had seen one hundred and fifty Labour MPs defect to the new entity, thus becoming the official opposition. Again, it might all still have crashed in the end anyhow, but it would have had a much better chance of achieving what it set out to achieve.

Lesson one: if you're going to split, you have to do it in very large numbers.

In a very odd sort of a way, the SDP actually did accomplish all it set out to at its creation – other than have the new party replace Labour as the dominant one of the British centre left, obviously. Crucially, the SDP wanted to make it so that a party could beat the Tories in a general election with centrist ideas; Tony Blair basically took the SDP's policy platform and ideology then built them over the Labour infrastructure to create a machine that won three elections in a row and had people crowing about the end of the Conservative Party;

unthinkable only a decade previous, when Mrs Thatcher seemed unstoppable. In essence, the SDP won the 1997, 2001 and 2005 general elections, and arguably the 2010 one as well. Cameron and Osborne looked up to Blair and wanted to infuse the Conservatives with social liberalism, making the party almost a fully liberal one in some senses. It didn't work out that way when they got into government, but the broad outline of that was still there in 2010.

By doing so, it changed politics, at least from the mid-'90s until the EU referendum, a not inconsiderable space of twenty years during which both Labour and the Conservative Party were doing their best SDP impressions (often to the chagrin of their backbenchers, which is why this glorious run had to come to an end eventually).

Lesson two: if it can be done, it's probably better to build your revolution over the top of one of the two major parties, rather than try to start something new.

The tension between these two lessons is the major reason why there has never been an SDP Mark 2, at least at the time of writing. But here's why the time may have come for a new party, in spite of the general election result making it all but practically impossible: we probably need some sort of SDP Mark 2 if for no other reason than to generate the new ideas that will actually solve the problems the country faces at the moment. Without the frisson of a new project, it might be next to impossible for the politicians of our time to do anything other than spin their wheels, living in constant fear of the electorate. It seems clear that both the Tories and Labour have hit some sort of a wall, both of them for different reasons, so someone else has to unlock British politics.

To state for the record once again, I realise that an SDP Mark 2 looks like a pipe dream after what just happened in the general election. But let us set aside the current political situation we all find ourselves in and dream a little, just for a moment. What were the problems the original SDP faced – and how could the Democratic Party overcome those obstacles if 2017 were more welcoming to such a project?

It is so important, this point, that I'll make it again: when the split occurs, make sure you take enough MPs with you that the new entity, whatever it is called, *has the numbers to become the official opposition at the very least.* If you don't have the MPs to achieve this, then there is no point in splitting; the plot will definitely fail. By becoming the official opposition (or the government) and then using that platform effectively, a new party could reasonably quickly replace Labour in the minds of voters as the only party that could possibly become a government other than the Tories.

If a majority of Labour MPs left Labour and created

the SDP Mark 2, it would take with it most of the parliamentary party by default and almost every single major donor,* which is a good start. All of the Labour members who have left over Corbyn's leadership as well as most of the Lib Dem base (who I believe would jump ship if it became clear this new centrist party was capable of winning an election) could give it a healthy membership, right off the bat. If the Democratic Party took with them the majority of the PLP, then this problem the original SDP faced would be eliminated.

That leaves the leadership problem to contend with. David Owen was a respected politician but was always too stern and dour to lead a movement and a party that needed to be about an optimistic alternative. To make matters worse, the split leadership in the Alliance was a disaster, with David Steel infamously parodied on *Spitting Image* as being hopelessly in thrall to the more assured Owen. The leadership conundrum would be one that the SDP Mark 2 would need to address upon inception, and would be their biggest obstacle to success, as it is the hardest of all of the SDP's old problems to solve in the modern day. There is no obvious candidate

---

* Jack Maidment, 'Labour donors "willing to fund new party in wake of a General Election defeat"', *Daily Telegraph*, 23 May 2017, accessed 10 August 2017 at: http://www.telegraph.co.uk/news/2017/05/23/labour-donors-willing-fund-new-party-wake-general-election-defeat/

in the current PLP that jumps out at you to assume this role. Yvette Cooper and Dan Jarvis would be fine to take over the Labour Party as caretakers, people who would steady the ship after the insanity of the Corbyn era, but neither is ideal to lead a new party that needs to get people's attention immediately. Chuka Umunna could grow into the role; but the issue is that he might not be given enough time to do so in what would quickly become a sink-or-swim situation. David Miliband could probably do it, given the 'prince across the water' image he's established in the media since he went to America, and given how much more assured he's become as a public figure since the 2010 leadership contest. But he is not currently a Member of Parliament and has repeatedly stated that he does not want to return to the Commons, trading in his enviable life in the States to do so. There is always the by-election route, but if you wanted to do that early in this new centrist party's life so that Miliband could assume leadership of the new party quickly, you'd face the problem of the SDP Mark 2 not having established itself in the minds of the public, and thus David Miliband might actually lose this by-election.

The SDP never really worked out who it was for, either. While Labour remained the party of the working man and the Tories the party of the wealthy and those who aspired to be so, it was hard for the SDP to pitch itself, as it wasn't clear who it was pitching itself to exactly. This is a problem the Lib Dems have inherited. Who would you bring together under this new big tent? One group would be the London vote I spoke of earlier, but that isn't enough to build a parliamentary majority on, and besides, this will likely be the last bastion of the Labour vote for years to come, no matter what happens, due to brand loyalty. The new party would have to have a pitch to older voters, and a lot of this could be built around social care, as it is an issue the Tories notably left themselves exposed on during the general election campaign. The business community is ripe for a switch from the Conservatives, with the anti-business rhetoric of the brief but memorable May-dominance period coupled with the debate around exiting the European Union leaving many business people disenchanted. Farmers are very likely to be given a raw deal in the Brexit negotiations – promises of keeping subsides at EU levels are already being prepared by the government to be broken. Young people are increasingly socially and economically liberal, as mentioned in the previous chapter. Think how hard it is to find an agenda that would bring those disparate groups together under one banner!

As if all these problems weren't enough, a new version of the SDP would face two huge additional challenges that are particular to 2017, one of which could be even bigger than the leadership problem, even if you could somehow get to a place where MPs were willing to leave the two big parties.

The most likely high-profile backers of this new party are Tony Blair, Peter Mandelson, Nick Clegg, George Osborne and ex-New Labour donors. These are all figures with considerable baggage, and some are amongst the most vilified figures in our current body politic. Were any combination of these people to front a new political party, the right-of-centre press would mercilessly rip it to shreds, doing what they did to the Lib Dems after the coalition was formed so successfully: shoving them into no-man's land, against the might of the Conservative Party and its associated press on one side and the still tribal Labour vote and media on the other. That's before we even get to Brexit, covered already in detail in Part I. An SDP Mark 2 would need to be about a hell of a lot more than reversing Brexit, or it would fail immediately.

Again, this is all fantasy talk, isn't it? No MP is going to leave the Labour Party after seeing the power of the brand in action – and no Conservative MP is going to leave the Tories now that doing so could bring on a general election and with it a Corbyn premiership. Or maybe, just maybe, we live in turbulent enough times politically that the prospect of a new, centrist, liberal party might not look as mad in a year or so's time as it appears right now. Maybe, just maybe, the infighting within the Conservative Party could become so great that the Tories really do split, providing a home for Labour moderates in the process, all of them united by getting behind a soft Brexit to start with it and taking it from there.

I'll leave you with one slightly insane scenario, one I absolutely do not think will happen but which, nonetheless, can't be totally discounted in the odd times we inhabit. Imagine it is early autumn of 2018 and no transitional deal with the EU Commission has been agreed. Theresa May is still Prime Minister and under pressure from the right of her party to let the clock run out so that we end up with no deal. The EU Commission announces a date when construction of border posts will go up between the north and south of Ireland. In light of all this, enough Tory and Labour MPs split off and form a 'coalition in the country's interest', supported by Lib Dems and the SNP, the aim of which is to reverse Article 50 and halt Brexit, at least for the time being. They challenge Theresa May's premiership directly, saying they are the only contingent that can command a majority in Parliament.

A new centrist party is needed. But for all the reasons I've just outlined, it's birth would be a messy one.

CHAPTER 22

HOW THE TORIES COULD STRIKE BACK

The first movie I was ever taken as a child to see was *Star Wars*, and by that I mean the original 1977 film which has since been rechristened *Star Wars Episode IV: A New Hope*. As a result, while I do not want to give the impression that I'm the sort of bloke who still has a Yoda duvet cover while drifting into his mid-forties, I do have a tendency to think in *Star Wars*-related metaphors a lot more than I probably should.

For instance, I have on occasion considered the merits, or lack thereof, of joining the Conservative Party. I have worked with (and continue at present to work with) people who are Tory members and I have liked almost all of them. I've also met Tories I wasn't keen on, but I can say the same thing about any classification of people by political affiliation, and the Conservatives in the bunch still come out pretty well. There is also a sort of Matthew Parris wing of the Conservative Party that I suppose I could probably fit into, and so it isn't that surprising that in the midst of all of the political disappointments of the past few years an 'if you can't beat 'em, join 'em' motif has occasionally occurred to me.

Yet every time my inner Tory attempts to assert itself, a *Star Wars*-related thing kicks in and cuts the whole thing dead. I live in Zone 2 London, and for a period of time my next-door neighbour was a feckless drunk who would spend hours standing outside of his own front door racially heckling passers-by. Watching this unfold, I would get to thinking things like, 'I can't believe this useless booze-hound gets to live in government housing while families have to work so hard just to get ahead in life, the welfare state is out of control, blah, blah...'

Then, as soon as these thoughts entered my brain, my frontal lobe would redirect itself to an image of the Tory MP Peter Bone, dressed as Emperor Palpatine in *Return of the Jedi*. Peter would be laughing that evil, Palpatine laugh and then say: 'Good, goooood! Use your aggressive feelings, boy; let the hate flow through you! Use your anger and your fear and your conversion to the Conservative Party will be complete!'

This is, of course, unfair on the Tories, but I suppose this sort of thought pattern is hardwired into my brain. I'll always respect the Tories but I still find it hard to feel I can join the Empire. If you want to know how the rest of this *Star Wars*-related analogy goes, here it is: Labour is like the Ewoks. From a distance, they look like cute teddy bears, but up close they tend to be vicious and somewhat feral. If you aren't one of them, they may just stick you on a spit and cook you for dinner. Given their cuddly exterior, they often get underestimated, but their fierce adherence to collectivism means they are a formidable force. They brought down the galactic Empire with some sticks and ropes, if you will recall. The Lib Dems are like the Jedi from the original trilogy because there used to be a lot of them all over the galaxy but now there are about two of them in total because something went very badly wrong with the leadership.

Space opera fun aside, there has been an overcorrection in the way both the Tories and Labour are now being thought and talked about in the media since the 2017 general election. Before the election, Labour were finished and the Tories were going to be in government for ever; now it is just a matter of waiting for the Conservatives to collapse and Corbyn will be Prime Minister, simple as that. I'll throw a wrench into those spokes here and now and say that while it looks much less likely than it did in April that we'll have a Tory government for the next ten years, not only is there every chance this will still be the case, *I would still say it is the most likely scenario*. Here's why.

The Tories, as they aptly demonstrated in putting together a minority government on the hoof after the setback of the election result, are very good in adverse situations. Labour, on the other hand, have a tendency to blow it and get cocky before No. 10 has been occupied for real (think 1992 or 2015 for reference). I'll stop right here and be really counterintuitive: there is nothing to suggest that the Tories might not be in power for the rest of time. And I don't use 'the rest of time' as hyperbole either – there is no hard and fast rule that says at some point another party has to displace the one currently ruling in a parliamentary democracy. In other words, the centre left, liberals, everyone on the non-Tory side of the political equation needs to get out of this Ed Miliband-esque, 35 per cent strategy way of thinking, as well as the 'Jeremy needs one last heave' mentality, which is all about waiting for the Tories to screw up somehow and then everyone votes for your bunch in desperation. It may work out for you; then again, it very much may not. People actually tend to stick with the status quo until both the status quo screws up and at the exact same time there happens to be an attractive alternative; whether we are there yet is very open to interpretation. In the meantime, so long as the Tories can keep the ship together and keep the government afloat, time is on their side. They can wait for the cracks to appear in the Labour Party again, which they will, and in fact the early warning signs are already visible, as I detailed in Part I.

I want to be clear that I'm not making a prediction here. There is nothing inevitable about Labour not forming a government again after the next general election by any means. What I'm saying is that the natural state of things as they stand is for the Tories to be in government for the rest of time when you consider all of the factors involved. In order for that not to be the case, I think something else needs to happen and it probably will require Labour to be proactive in some way. The left needs to stop relying on the right screwing up and power landing in their laps by default.

For of all of the bad habits of the left I outlined in Part III of this book, the one I neglected to touch upon was the tendency of progressives to convince themselves that things are going fine, great even, when in actual fact they are going either not so great or even terribly and another defeat to the right is inevitable. Lib Dems are particularly bad at this, but then again, Labour were the ones who bought into the 35 per cent strategy for almost an entire parliament, and how many people who had said Corbyn was a disaster over and over again are now convinced he's the real deal, all because he avoided catastrophe? There is a bias towards hope over adversity on the left side of the political axis. This can be good and it can be bad. It is good to keep heart when all seems lost. It is bad to tell yourself you are going to beat the Tories when you're still six points behind them in the most favourably biased election polls, and then to claim victory when the Tories are still in government afterwards.

Another really bad habit that the left of centre tends to adopt is the search for purity. The 2015 Labour leadership contest was pretty much all about this factor exclusively, and you can look at any aspect of that contest if you want to understand this phenomenon. The right, meanwhile, tends to focus on obtaining power much more single-mindedly; this is exactly why they are better at it. Here's something no one in progressive politics says enough: there is no 'pure' solution to the world's or the country's problems. There are just principles to follow. Like liberalism: we believe that people should be free to decide their own destinies as much as possible. Or social democracy: sometimes, achieving the liberalism we desire requires the state to get involved where markets have either failed or aren't built to provide for certain needs. But then how you achieve that should be left open to argument. The left has way, way, way too many shibboleths, which is why it spends all its energy being against things as opposed to being for things. This is still a problem for Labour, post-surge or not.

The general election didn't hold out much hope for progressive parties, when all of the fantasy stuff is put to one side, but there was one thing we did find out: the Tories are actually pretty beatable. Yet so long as non-Tory parties continue with their bad habits, the Conservatives can continue to keep winning by default.

On the hard left, the Conservatives being in power is oddly not viewed as such a bad thing. Or rather, it is viewed as being less bad in terms of eventual outcomes than liberal rule, due to the fact that the liberals will supposedly keep things just ticking along whereas the right will inevitably cause a crisis which will in turn cause a backlash that will make people break out of 'false consciousness' and come to the conclusion that socialism is the only option. The whole of the Corbyn project is, in actuality, based on this premise; this is why gaining real power would be fatal to it, something no one on the left seems to have twigged in the shadow of the general election result that didn't go as planned for Theresa May.

The reality of what long-term Tory rule would do to anything in the progressive sphere is somewhat different. For a start, Conservative rule when looked at historically is largely self-sustaining. Even when Tory governments do something significantly wrong or are faced with an external crisis, this tends to cause fear to rise in the populace, and when people feel afraid, they vote in greater numbers for the conservative option. As it could well be with Brexit, regardless of how it actually turns out. Get it right and they are credited by the electorate for having done something well; if it goes badly, then it looks like we need the Tories to steer the ship through the crisis. The problems with Brexit might all end up being the EU's fault anyhow, in the minds of the British electorate. Again, the left cannot hope to win simply because the Tories lose.

As mentioned already, the Conservative Party only really falls from power when it has both wildly misjudged the prevailing mood of the general public and done so at a time when a credible opposition leader was in place. In the past century, this has only happened three times: in 1945, when the Conservatives underestimated the public's appetite for greater public services following VE Day; in 1964, when it failed to recognise British society's emerging liberalism; and in 1997, when it again failed to understand the new liberalism then emerging in society and were out of step with it. This could be why Corbyn failed to win in 2017: they had policies that resounded with the public, but didn't have a leader that enough people thought was up to the job.

This suggests the strength of the Conservatives' ability to hold onto power once they get into office. It certainly doesn't help that the Labour Party tends to fall into chaos the moment that happens, but it has a lot more to do with the actual Conservative Party and how it operates than that. Amongst other attributes, it is interesting how adaptable the party is. Look at Theresa May's switch from light Remainer to hard-line Brexiteer as a good example. Within Labour or Lib Dem circles, such a change of mind on the major topic of the day would be considered heresy. Or, even better still, let us revisit this soon-to-be-buried passage from the 2017 Tory manifesto, the one under which Britain is still currently technically governed: 'We do not believe in untrammelled free markets. We reject the cult of selfish individualism. We abhor social division, injustice, unfairness and inequality.'*

The manifesto even has an entire section entitled 'We believe in the good that government can do'. This is a change of direction very profound for the party of Thatcher, one that has caused the economic right of the party to get wound up, particularly given this policy strategy did not even net the party the large majority it was supposed to have done. All this causes one to

---

* Conservative Party manifesto, 'Our principles', 2017 general election

remember just how precarious a place the Conservative Party is in at present, with the DUP having to support them in Parliament simply to make up a very slender majority. But it also reminds us again just how quickly and sensibly the Tories responded to the unexpected situation they found themselves in after the 2017 general election. A government at the ready, the Queen's Speech delayed by nothing more than twenty-four hours. The fury so many Tory MPs must have had regarding Theresa May's reckless and self-centred gamble – yet they knew that keeping her in place for the time being was the only way to steady the ship enough to avoid another general election, one that would probably have been disastrous for them. It is only the flexibility of the Conservative Party ideologically, combined with the hunger for power, that made all this possible.

The left will not simply inherit power; they must pursue it in a realistic fashion. This is precisely what they are not doing presently, which is why they still have major problems to contend with.

CHAPTER 23

IMAGINING THE FIRST YEAR OF A CORBYN-LED LABOUR GOVERNMENT

8 May 2020. The nation is waking up to a not entirely surprising Labour victory in the general election that was called after the government finally fell under the weight of its own contradictions. The Tory–DUP government had managed to limp on through the initial two years of negotiations with the EU around leaving the European Union; all that two-year process achieved was working out a transitional deal that would be in place indefinitely. The deal in question basically turns Britain into Norway, but with the added wrinkle of being inside of the customs union – Norway+ it has been dubbed by the *Financial Times* and *The Economist*, referring to it positively; the *Mail* and *The Sun*, use the same term,

only pejoratively. Freedom of movement remains mostly the same as a result, despite the government using the emergency brake feature for a period. Resentment about this amongst Leave voters has been a factor in Labour's victory, particularly as the party managed to get almost all of the Remain, pro-immigration voters at the same time, miraculously successfully continuing their Janus routine on the Brexit issue, this time all the way to a parliamentary majority. The near total collapse of the SNP (now down to a mere eight seats) means that Labour's decade-long slide in Scotland has been dramatically halted, with the party taking more than thirty-five seats north of the border. Labour's thirty-odd seat majority has come not just at the expense of the Tories and the Nats, but the Lib Dems as well, who have lost every single seat previously held in the House of Commons, wiped out as a parliamentary force entirely.

The Conservatives had, of course, been desperate to stave off a general election, but a series of by-elections triggered by pro-Brexit Tory MPs walking off in a huff after the transitional deal had been signed, and those by-elections being subsequently won by the Labour Party, destroyed David Davis's razor-thin majority. The election unavoidable, the Tories decided to run towards it as opposed to cowering in fear; Davis called the election and asked Labour to support, knowing that with

Corbyn's party polling around 50 per cent, their votes to bring down the Parliament were inevitable.

Early on in the contest, it looked like the Tories might even be able to hang on. Davis's working-class roots were played up endlessly to compare with Corbyn's upper-middle-class ones, giving the Conservatives a brief but notable surge, and the parties were neck and neck in the polls for a week or so. But as election day approached, it became clear to everyone that Labour were pulling ahead.

The day after the 2020 general election is mayhem. Davis resigns as Tory leader, but not after having been begged to stay on for a few months as Leader of the Opposition by a good number of his MPs, just to steady the ship. Meanwhile, ecstatic street parties break out in most major cities as young people act like the revolution has arrived and all of their worries have been calmed for ever. Corbyn addresses a large crowd in Hyde Park the day after the election, at a hastily arranged concert/celebration rally. From the stage, Corbyn announces a 'new dawn' for the country, telling the boisterous crowd that 'the age of austerity is over', to massive cheers. Objectively speaking, of course, the age of austerity had been over for a few years already. The Tories, in a desperate bid to cling to power, had begun bribing the public long ago, putting into law as many of Corbyn's desired goodies as could be reasonably afforded. It had all been to no avail.

Corbyn gives another speech to a mass of people assembled in Trafalgar Square later that same day under the banner of 'Make May the end of Davis', which, although a small point in the grand scheme of things, is a very much less catchy slogan than the rally held after the previous general election had going for it.

'We have won!' he says to loud cheers. 'YOU have won!' gets an even bigger noise from the assembled. They will all tell their grandchildren they were here on this great day, when peace in Britain finally descended for good. Meanwhile back in the real world, the markets have crashed with the onset of Labour's victory, and the pound has dropped along with them, achieving parity with the American dollar. Newspapers like the *Financial Times* wonder how Corbyn is going to pay for all the stuff he promised in his manifesto, particularly given it had even more giveaways crammed into it than the 2017 manifesto contained (they were pretty sure of victory, but wanted to make sure, you see). Not only free tuition fees promised for everyone, but a very generous maintenance grants scheme; free childcare, all day long, for every child between three and six; £30 billion to be pledged to the NHS, every year; the triple lock to be supplemented with pay-outs to those who had been hit in recent years by the pension age rising, particularly women; a pledge to renationalise the railways, water and energy grid. The IFS had already called the whole package wildly unaffordable during the election campaign, and when inflation and the sinking pound are priced in, it is even more so now – so what will Corbyn prioritise, the sensible heads across the nation ask? For the time being, Corbyn insists in all interviews that everything promised in the manifesto will go ahead.

The new Cabinet contains no surprises, with John McDonnell going to No. 11, Diane Abbott to the Home Office and Emily Thornberry to the FCO. But the Queen's Speech is an odd affair, one that includes the NHS spending pledge, the renationalisation of the railways plan (but no other renationalisation), the maintenance grants policy – but, notably, not the abolition of tuition fees. Anger at the free tuition fees pledge being rescinded hits *The Guardian*; in the weeks that follow the Queen's Speech, it becomes clear that the Labour government intends on sticking with the coalition policy on post-secondary fees, at least for the time being. Corbyn pretends for a bit as if there was no reneging on the manifesto promise, but that is unsustainable, even for him. In a BBC News interview, he tells the public that Labour still wants to abolish tuition fees – just not just yet.

'Give us time to do everything we said we were going to do. Don't worry, it's all going to happen, and soon.'

The left buys this, for now, still upset at the tuition fees staying as is but not yet ready to protest Corbyn and a Labour government they are still in love with.

Also missing is the free childcare promise, causing lots of mumbles on Mumsnet but little else. John McDonnell tells the nation free childcare is an 'aspiration' of the Labour government and something they will 'get to eventually'. He says that the priorities in these 'hard times' must be to improve the NHS and to maintain welfare spend, playing on middle-class guilt. McDonnell says that good times are 'around the corner' and that the markets will improve very shortly. The middle-class left doesn't feel able to moan, at least not yet.

Unfortunately for everyone, the markets do not improve, and in fact get worse as the months roll on. The borrowing for the NHS spend causes problems for the Treasury as they try to classify it as capital spend as opposed to day-to-day. The end result is that Standard & Poor reassess the UK's credit rating, from the AA held prior to the election down to A-. Fitch goes further and downgrades Britain's credit rating to BBB, meaning the UK now has the creditworthiness of Colombia. This makes it much harder for the UK to borrow at decent rates – and makes the NHS spending pledged in the

Queen's Speech seem doubtful. Corbyn sticks to the notion that it will all be fine.

'We promised to spend £30 billion a year on the NHS and that is precisely what we intend to do.'

Despite the government coming under increased pressure due to this financial storm, Corbyn himself seems more Monsieur Zen than ever. He appears on *The One Show* with seeming regularity, hardly talking about politics at all during these spots, but taking the time to discuss the latest grime albums he apparently appreciates, as well as the manhole covers he has been collecting (the latter with more obvious authenticity than the former). While the right-wing tabloids scream blue murder and the right-leaning broadsheets supply endless analyses of how we're headed for the mother of all crises, Labour's poll ratings remain in the mid-forties, the Tories lagging, four, five, six points behind them.

Then comes the winter, and a real crisis in the NHS causes the first wobble in public opinion. A young woman dies while waiting for treatment in an A&E department due to an overlong waiting time. Questions are asked about the money being poured into the NHS to no visible improvement, particularly as all of the money is going there instead of funding free tuition fees and childcare. This leads to the press digging further and discovering an NHS in deep crisis. Corbyn handles an interview about it all very badly, trying to blame it all on the last Conservative government. The nation watches the long-awaited return of 'crabby Corbyn', the guy who hates being questioned by the press and responds by being grumpy.

The 2021 Queen's Speech ends months of speculation about what will happen to tuition fees: not only are they going to remain where they are, the maintenance grant schemes rolled out the previous year are to be rolled back as well. This is the red line crossed for the NUS, which organises a large protest in London. Signs are seen with things like 'Corbyn – where did our love go?' with a picture of Corbyn's face broken in half upon an equally broken heart. The tuition fees protest turns out be a breaking-the-seal moment, as protests against the government become larger, more organised and more regular. Corbyn tries his avuncular charm to win back the kids, but when that doesn't work he does his usual Plan B and scorns them all, hiding from the press and becoming a virtual recluse in his house in Islington (he never took up residence in No. 10, leading to a great many problems in the running of the government that were papered over at first).

A recession kicks in, the first proper one in years, with growth expected to fall to minus 2 per cent for 2021 overall. The UK's credit rating is downgraded again, with Standard & Poor giving it a BBB. The Labour poll numbers go into freefall, with the Tories suddenly back to Theresa May pre-general election 2017 levels and Labour in the mid-twenties again. The Lib Dems make a comeback of sorts, getting into double figures for the first time in years.

Corbyn not only starts to avoid the domestic press, but begins sending Thornberry in his place to things like G8 summits, NATO summits and – particularly – anything involving having to interact in anyway with Donald Trump. Soon enough, he has McDonnell fill in at PMQs, leading to tricky constitutional questions. Rumours begin to circulate about Corbyn's health, with the lieutenants offered up for media spots in his stead constantly having to say Jeremy is fine and in perfect health. This in turn makes a mockery of the excuses they try to offer for why he, the Prime Minister of the country, continues to avoid doing the basic portions of his job.

Corbyn finally quits as leader of the Labour Party just shy of a year since becoming Prime Minister, doing so via a pre-taped speech in which he acts as if he is reading something off a cue card at gunpoint. John McDonnell is 'named' as his successor, which causes all sorts of problems within the Labour Party, as the moderates realise instantly that Corbyn stepping down equals a chance, a slim but real chance, to regain control of the party.

Yvette Cooper stands against McDonnell in a contest that lasts just under three weeks. At the end of it, McDonnell is elected leader of the Labour Party, and by extension Prime Minister, with over 70 per cent of the vote. He wastes no time at all in enacting his intended programme, which he lays out in his acceptance speech: 'Jeremy's problem is that he was never radical enough. He was always at his core a bleeding-heart liberal, dedicated to socialism in principle but never willing to do the things it would take to make real socialism a reality. That's where I come in.'

A week later, McDonnell travels to Brussels to see the Commission. After a two-hour meeting, several of the key negotiators on the EU side come out looking pale, almost ill.

'The new British Prime Minister has said that he would like to end the transitional deal we had arranged with the previous British administration with immediate effect. All dealings between the European Union and the United Kingdom have now been officially terminated. "No deal" is a reality,' says Barnier to a room of stunned hacks and officials.

News of this development sends British youth into a frenzy. While protests against the Labour government had become common, they now go up several notches, with a massive protest in London converging on Hyde

Park one Saturday afternoon. However, the assembled students protesting in central London are in for a shock: mass riot police descend on the crowds, half of them beating the protestors, the other half rounding up as many of the kids as possible and throwing them into the back of police vans. The protest vanishes quickly, as those participants who haven't been beaten or detained realise that if they wish to avoid either fate they had better flee the scene and blend back into the general London populace as quickly as possible, abandoning their 'Jez We Can't' signs along the way.

Prime Minister McDonnell gives an interview with the BBC the following morning and is asked if the reaction to the protests was ordered by No. 10 directly.

'Yes, it was,' he answers dryly.

'Isn't that a breach of the human rights of those protestors who were beaten or arrested?'

'Human rights are an EU concept, and we are no longer part of the European Union.'

That same day, the BBC reporter who conducted the McDonnell interview is sacked. In fact, over the next week or so, there are mass involuntary redundancies at the BBC. Ironically, this is only covered by right-wing tabloids, and the government counters with the line that stories about the sackings are simply 'fake news'. As the month since McDonnell became Prime Minister progresses, the BBC is filled with new, young faces who seem to have nothing but a slightly creepy admiration for McDonnell first, and the Labour Party second.

'Leveson 3' comes into law very quickly via a statutory instrument of dubious legality, allowing the government to seize all property of the Murdoch press in surprisingly short order. Most newspapers go out of print, including *The Guardian*. At first, there is a sudden upsurge of bloggers reporting on what's actually happening (while the BBC becomes ever more like North Korean state television by the day), but this thins out quickly, with most blogs 'disappearing' suddenly, along with their authors.

Full-blown nationalism of industry is announced the following month, with previous owners of land and industry to receive 'some compensation' (which comes to mean, in reality, 'no compensation'). Everyone who can get out tries to do so; the British government responds by closing the borders, meaning no one can get in or out of the country for any reason. The army is redirected to patrol the coast, with orders to shoot on sight anyone trying to leave or enter the country.

It appears the socialist revolution has finally arrived in Britain.

CHAPTER 24

A GLANCE AHEAD TO CONSERVATIVE PARTY CONFERENCE, 2018

Iboard the train to Manchester with two hours to kill. My aim is to take the time to read a pretentious philosophical tome I've been promising myself I will tackle for ages, but instead I fall asleep pretty much as soon as we pull out of Euston. I dream about the last Tory conference that was held in Manchester, all the way back in good ol' 2017 (it was, torturously, a biennial event; now, even more frequent). About the guy wearing the orange 'Jeremy Ain't Nuthin' To Fuck With' T-shirt loitering outside, trying to pick a fight with anyone wearing a suit. About the gauntlet one had to run in order to get into the conference itself, complete with the danger of being pelted with plastic balls. On one journey into this pit of hate, I was standing right in front of a female minister when a scary-looking man lurched over the barrier and told her in no uncertain terms that he was intending to commit an illegal sexual act upon her if ever they were in close enough physical proximity to allow it. As he shouted this, he was cheered on by the women either side of him. 2015 was exactly the same and I have difficulty separating my memories of one from the other.

Now, I'm faced with back-to-back Manchester Tory conferences. Given that it's the Conservative Party, I get that they must be getting a great deal somehow and that the whole thing is thus transactional, but still, do they really not get that Manchester hates them? It's one of the only parts of the country that still does in that particularly visceral way, but that only makes the Mancs all the more vocal about it.

My dreams on the train then take me back to when I myself lived in Manchester, back in the late '90s. I moved there rather randomly, which made my experiences there even weirder than they would have otherwise been. I lived in Levenshulme, which back then was really pretty rough. One could live in that part of the world very inexpensively, though, and that was its own compensation. The local pub closest to my flat wanted to put up the price of a pint of bitter from £1.05 to £1.08 at one point. A petition went round which managed to keep the real ale at a pound and five pence a pop. Everyone called each other 'comrade' and the worst thing you could call anyone, ever, was a Tory. Despite the grumbles about New Labour (even then), voting for anyone other than Labour was tantamount to treason against the Republic of Mancunia. Whenever people have told me over the years that the Labour Party will be finished soon enough, I remember those days up north and tell them to not be so certain.

I awaken from my dreams about my late '90s existence to find the train has just stopped in Stoke-on-Trent. Some well-dressed men in their early twenties get on board; one of them sees how I'm dressed and gives me a nod. They begin to talk amongst themselves in north Midlands accents about the conference they are on their way to, for what turns out to be the first time for all of them. Excited young Tories from the northern Midlands, what a concept. When the train pulls into Manchester Piccadilly, I grab my stuff and do my usual double-take while walking through the station. Back when I lived in Manchester, Piccadilly station was perhaps the worst place in Europe, populated with heroin addicts, LSD victims and mobile phones sales people. No one who congregated there for purposes other than to board a train ever seemed to leave, other than to take the short walk down the hill to Piccadilly Gardens to urinate in the open square. These days, said piazza has been magically transformed into the kind of place you'd actually want to spend time in voluntarily. All paid for with EU money, of course, like most other things that are not crap in the north of England.

It isn't long before I have to find a way to get to my hotel without crossing a picket line. The whole of central Manchester has become the battlefield it always is when the Tories are in town, only now, after the Labour surge in the general election and that sense the left still has the wind behind its back, the protests have gone up a notch in terms of numbers, intensity and the general threat of violence. I feel self-conscious in my suit and suddenly curse myself for having not dressed casually and then changed when I got to my hotel.

'Oi, there's a Tory!' one of the guys marching while holding a trade union banner says, causing my stomach to lurch, but he laughs straight after, calming my nerves. I get to the hotel in one piece and steel myself for the corridor of doom that one has to brave in order to get into the conference hall itself.

Turns out, the entrance is much better policed than last year, or 2015 for that matter, which is good because there are about three times as many people protesting outside as there were then, and all of them are about four times angrier than they were last year. I try to block it out, but it is hard to do so fully as the screams are so viscerally hateful. I count my blessings that at least I hadn't run into the guy in the orange T-shirt trying to pick fights.

Inside, of course, it's like being in a parallel universe to the Manchester I've just left outside. Half the Cabinet stand perched at the Midland's bar; every lobbyist in the country skirts around, hoping to grab the MP they had promised to have a chat with now so that they can enjoy the receptions all night, carefree; the earnest, left-wing end of the NGO world huddles together for warmth at two tables in the corner, hating every minute of this yearly ritual their professions call upon them to undertake. I spot a journalist I know and make small talk.

'Busy this year,' he says.

'It's still the one that matters.'

'Labour was awful again this year, wasn't it?'

'What were you expecting?'

'I don't know. Not that. God, let's get a drink.'

At the bar, several junior ministers complain about Brussels. My journalist friend and I are joined by a backbencher who is a mutual acquaintance.

'Had a job coming to me if we'd won properly in 2017,' the MP says with a self-deprecating shrug. 'Now I think it's all passed me by.'

'There will be more reshuffles,' I say.

'No, there won't be,' says the journalist, meaning for his sardonic quip to be funny, but it falls flat. We all sip our lager in peace for the moment.

The conference hall is its usual ideal place to catch up on your sleep, just like it is every year. At least during the coalition years it was fun to watch Tory Cabinet ministers have to veer between the sensible portions of their speeches and the nutty bits of flesh for the activists to chew on. I remember one conference when William Hague was Foreign Secretary, and his speech was putting the activists into slumber with its talk of NATO summits and UN initiatives when he paused for a moment, made the sort of face one makes just before they are about to take a shot of hard liquor, and said in a decibel range notably higher, 'And we're not going to get the answer by listening to those Eurocrats in Brussels!' Suddenly, the crowd came to life, roaring with approval. The energy level tapered off again when Hague returned to Planet Earth, but it was fun while it lasted. These days, everyone wants to steer clear of discussing Brussels if at all possible when on the conference stage, sadly, leaving no room for the activists to have an enjoyable moment.

I have a fringe event to chair in the afternoon. At 2016 conference, it was almost impossible to attend a fringe event that didn't have 'Brexit' in the title; this year, like its absence in the hall, no one wants to talk about Europe all of a sudden. The fringe I'm chairing has to do with the economy, and whether or not the Tories have become communists these days. We end with a speech from a Tory MP who was part of the small 2017 intake, one newly enraptured with social democracy of a Toryish kind, who ends up quoting Churchill. It causes me to smile when I recall that it was something he said while he was a Liberal.

Work done, there is little to do now but go from reception to reception, drinking the free booze. For a while under Cameron, the level of posh alcohol available for free was reined in. Now, with the fear of a country being run by Jeremy Corbyn in the air, it's like Caligula's Rome. After I shave off some caviar from a statue of Edward Heath made from fish eggs, I scan the room for familiar faces. As I am doing so, I am accosted by someone I would have preferred to avoid, a particularly irksome in-house public affairs bore.

'Hey, Ty-man…'

Ty-man?

'…looks like you got the election result, pretty, pretty wrong there.'

'As did everyone else in the universe.'

'You were only one who predicted the Le Pen win, though.'

'I was trying to make a broader point when I said I thought Le Pen would win.'

'It was an artistic statement, was it?'

'Sort of.'

'She still didn't win though.'

'Which I was happy about!'

I'm about to walk off when he stops me and gets down to business. He wants an introduction to a recently promoted minister (promoted beyond his station, if you ask me, but that's an aside) and I oblige, figuring it will allow me to float into a circle that looks worth being part of anyhow. It is a group of mostly backbench MPs complaining about Nick Timothy and the 'lurch towards socialism' that was apparently the reason for the hung parliament.

'It's coming to the point where you have to ask yourself what is the point in even being a Tory any longer when we behave as we do in government,' one member of the 1922 Committee says to no one in particular but really to everyone in earshot.

'Eight years we've had a Conservative Prime Minister and yet look at the socialism we continue to foster,' says another, shaking his head. I know what's coming: the big topic.

'And she destroyed Brexit along the way,' one of the MPs says. This is met with mumbles of discontent from several in the circle. In the meantime, I've got to talking with a very famous media journalist who just happened to be standing nearby. An old hat at this, I fall into conversation with him by pretending that we're on familiar terms. You see, very well-known political TV journos have met so many people over the years that if you act like they should by rights know very well who you are, they simply play along. This very famous television journalist casually drops into conversation that he can get me into a very, very exclusive party containing most of the Cabinet. I play it as cool as one can do in such a circumstance.

'Oh yes, that one,' I say to him. 'I was going to go to that anyway, so let's wander over together.'

I've just done something completely stupid, and the idiocy of it smacks me in the face as we're on our way to the party: I am relying on the very famous television journalist to get me into the party while having told him beforehand that I was on the guest list. Fortunately, it all works out for me.

'You have to let this man in,' says the famous television journalist. 'He's the most vital man in the whole country!'

This, rather oddly, because it isn't how these things usually work, manages to actually get me through the door. I can't leave to take a piss or I'll never get back inside, but at least I'm now in. Of course, victory on these fronts at Tory conference are always short-lived; you're standing there with your glass of complimentary bubbles in hand, congratulating yourself on having schmoozed a famous television journalist to talk you into an exclusive party, only to find someone you hold in contempt standing in the exact same position. And here stand several such creatures, all Westminster bottom feeders, all quaffing free champagne. Thankfully, most of them are clustered together, like penguins trying to avoid the Antarctic frost.

'Join us, Ty-man!'

I smile and move past them, jogging towards a high end-looking circle of people, mostly Cabinet members. I try to blend in but mostly fail to do so. After a while I drop out and finally get even more drunk while talking to some journalist friends.

It's late by this stage – very late – and I have a funny moment where I panic about having to be up to get the kids dressed and ready for school, before realising I'm on the road and don't have to worry about it on this rare occasion. Of course, this makes me miss my kids terribly all of a sudden, and I pick up my phone with an urge to call my wife and tell her to wake up the kids so I can have a chat with them. Thankfully, noting that it is 1.42 in the morning makes me realise this is a terrible idea, one I abandon instantly.

The only thing still open is Beers of Europe, but hey, it's free beer, so what the hell. I suck on an Efes looking for friends, but everyone's a stranger. I have one of those moments you only get at Conservative Party conference: one minute you're rubbing shoulders with the upper echelons of the political class, the next you're involved in a wild, apocalyptic hunt for lager, wondering where it all went wrong in your life.

It's very much the wee hours now, and my thoughts surreally turn to a flyer I was once handed in Amsterdam, years and years ago now, in regards to the nightclub it was advertising: open 4 a.m. 'til late. I'm much drunker than I promised myself I would become and suddenly filled with regret. It happens every year at Tory conference; it's all free and delicious and you always consume too much of it all. I wander around the now empty conference hallways and back out into a Manchester that's colder than I was expecting. This moment always makes you empathetic for what Cinderella must have felt when the coach turned back into a pumpkin. At least it's a short walk to my hotel.

'Oi, Tory boy!'

I turn around to locate the voice that just shouted this in my direction. What I see makes my blood run cold: it is the man in the orange T-shirt. I know it is, because it looks exactly like him and he is actually wearing the shirt in question. Now it is just he and I, alone on the streets of Manchester. I steel myself for the physical violence I figure must be inevitable now, thanking God for small miracles that at least I'll be too drunk to feel it all properly. He stops just short of me.

'Which way are you headed?' he asks me convivially.

'This way,' I say and start walking. We begin strolling together, side by side. I figure he's going to try to mug me or something, but at least every step gets me closer to the hotel and raises my chances of getting out of this situation no worse off.

'Had a bit to drink tonight, have we?' he asks me.

'Yes,' I respond honestly, trying to sound as friendly and unfazed as I possibly can.

'Me too. Me too. Not champagne, mind, but a lot of Holt's bitter.'

'I would rather have been drinking Holt's all night,' I tell him honestly.

'Ah well, you should have been down the pub then instead of inside the Midland with all them posh blokes.'

'Had to be there for work.'

'Where do you work then?'

'I work for a charity,' I tell him, which is at least true in context (I'm there representing a charitable organisation).

'So, you're not actually a Tory then?' he asks, as if

working for a charity and being a member of the Conservative Party were mutually exclusive things.

'No, I'm not.'

'That's funny, mate.'

And at this point he really does begin to laugh. In fact, so much so that he needs to pause for a moment. I think briefly about running for it, but the hotel is still a bit of a walk away and I feel almost certain the exertion would make me vomit. Besides, curiosity has got the better of me at this stage.

'Why's that so funny?'

'Because that means of the two of us, I'm the only Tory.'

'Huh?' I ask.

'I voted Tory in the general election.'

'Was it the first time you'd voted Tory?'

I begin walking again. He gets the hint and catches up.

'It was the first time I'd ever voted, period.'

'There is the obvious question for me to ask you now, of course.'

'Because it felt like the thing I wasn't supposed to do. The thing that was forbidden.'

'You voted Tory to rebel?'

'I suppose I did.'

'Why are you still wearing that T-shirt then?'

'If I took it off, all my mates would ask me why I wasn't

wearing it any more and then they might be able to sniff out what I'd done.'

'I see your point. Do you regret voting Tory?'

He looks around him at this point, worried about who might be in earshot. The coast is clear.

'No, actually. It felt pretty good. I think I'd do it again.'

When we reach my hotel, I walk inside and orange T-shirt-wearing, secret Tory man does not follow me. We don't even say goodnight to one another.

The next morning, I feel terrible. Tory conference hangovers are like no other, for reasons I've never been able to work out. Particularly the one you get at the end of Conservative Party conference, as it is the last one on the docket; it's like a cumulative hangover, coming off the back of the ones you had after the Lib Dems and after Labour. But you also feel a bit bad for having Toried it up a little too much. For the times you found yourself saying, after far too much complimentary wine, 'I suppose we do need to stop the poor sucking off the state', wondering where the hell the right-wing banter came from exactly. You depressingly realise that you are influenced by your surroundings far more than you tend to recognise.

The one last piece of business is to watch the Prime Minister's speech. There have been rumours of all sorts swirling around for weeks regarding what she might say, and I haven't found any of them convincing. I can't face the cordon of doom, never mind the conference hall beyond it, so I find a pub to watch it in. About midway through, the key moment comes: 'Therefore, I believe the Conservative Party requires my leadership throughout the whole of the Brexit process, and I vow to fight on as your Prime Minister...'

I get up to leave at this point, wishing to beat the rush even further. At the train station, I manage to spill a yogurt all over the floor of Pret A Manger, a visceral event that shocks my nervous system still, even as Manchester rolls away behind me. I realise there's no way I'm going to survive this journey without some hair of the dog inside of me; I retreat to the buffet car for a can of lager. I dunk it down like it is medicine; thankfully, it does the trick and I'm soon asleep, dreaming about William Hague being stuck in a never-ending loop of that little breath that prefaced the loony portions of his conference speeches, the red meat for the activists that he always so clearly detested delivering.

On the bus back to my house, I think back on Labour conference and the amazing things I saw there: on stage, in the middle of a debate, a mass grouping of the PLP marching on stage, with Chuka coming to the microphone to announce the formation of the Democratic Party of Great Britain and Northern Ireland. The split had finally happened. I had felt good about it for most of the week afterwards; felt excited about British politics as opposed to let down, for the first time in a while. A few days at Tory conference have now brought me back down to Earth. As I cross the Thames, I think of the enormous mountain that needs to be climbed, of all those who have failed before, and genuinely fear for the strength of those trying to climb the mountain this time round.

CHAPTER 25

OK, SERIOUSLY, WHAT HAPPENS NEXT?

British politics is in an extremely dark place at present. During the course of this book, I hope I've successfully outlined just how bad things are for liberals in the United Kingdom as they stand. The political system is reverting from a multi-party arrangement to a two-party set-up, one in which the right-wing party is in flux but has recently taken a statist, socially conservative turn, while the left-wing party is very successfully attempting to turn itself into a fully socialist outfit. Brexit is on, and we're now in a position in which pro-European Brits need to be overjoyed if we end up out of the EU and remain in the EEA, a situation many of them once decried as being the worst of all worlds. Due to the election result, a new, breakaway centrist party looks further from being a possibility than ever. It can seem as if there is no one to support, and no hope of anything emerging that liberals and centrists can truly get behind.

Ten years ago, Euroscepticism was the preserve of a few oddball academics, some tinfoil hat merchants, the fascist right, and hard-left marginal loons such as Jeremy Corbyn. And yet through their persistence, they eventually won. They changed the country through sheer bloody-mindedness; had the hardcore ranks of Eurosceptics just given up hope, there's no way we would have had an EU referendum, no chance at all. They act as the strangest possible inspiration for the centrists of today: no matter how forlorn your cause seems, persistence will get you surprisingly far in politics, as in life in general.

What the Eurosceptics of back then had that the progressives of today do not is clarity of vision and purpose. What are progressives trying to achieve exactly? What sort of UK do progressives want to live in?

I've tried to answer these questions by coming up with a list of what I believe could be the next steps that liberals and centrists might take. This list is by no means definitive; it is meant to be the start of what I hope will be a long conversation.

1. Disrupt the Corbyn consensus within the Labour Party, however and whenever possible.

The Labour leader is the enemy of liberalism, now more than ever after an election that has been taken by many as a vindication of him and his approach. Labour certainly can't even begin to be a liberal, centrist party until this takes place. How this is done is much harder to prescribe – his hold on the party is pretty tight at present. If this cannot take place, then Labour really is finished as anything other than a hard-left vehicle from here on in.

2. Labour MPs should seriously consider a split, however messy or dangerous it appears to be.

Paul Mason, speaking at this year's Progress conference, urged moderates within the Labour Party to break away and form a new centrist party. Taunting the Blairites in the crowd, the left-wing commentator said:

> You are all welcome in Jeremy Corbyn's Labour Party. But if you want a centrist party, this is not going to be it for the next ten years.
>
> The question for people in this room is: it is now a left-wing Labour Party. It is a Labour Party led by a man vilified in fourteen pages of the *Daily Mail*, and *The Sun*,

as a 'terrorist sympathiser', and we got 13 million votes. Do you want to be part of it, or not?[*]

As much as many in that Progress crowd would disagree with Mason on many things (and he was, inevitably, booed), they may come to see his words as a clarion call in years to come. After all, as they don't want Corbyn to become Prime Minister in the end, they have little to lose. Ironically, it is the Labour left who do have something to forfeit should the party split in the ways Mason has suggested, seeing as how a split of the Labour Party could cause a split in the progressive vote, allowing the Tories to govern when they may not have been able to otherwise. If history repeats itself, however, it also means that at some point Labour becomes a centrist vehicle once again, whatever happens to the group that enacts the split in the first place. It happened with the SDP, and with Labour's subsequent adoption of Blairism, and it could go down mostly the same way once again.

The game is up. Labour moderates can be angry about it until the end of time if they wish, but the party has become the preserve of Corbyn and his road to nowhere. Starting a new party will take ten years to become successful if everything goes well, probably more like fifteen

---

[*] Paul Mason, Progress conference, panel discussion, 24 June 2017

or twenty, during which time the Conservative Party will be in power continuously. This has to be compared to the alternative should the moderates continue to fall silently in behind Jeremy Corbyn, hoping that someday the membership sees the light: that may well either keep the Conservative Party in power for the rest of eternity, or bring to power a Labour government that would be a disaster for the country.

3. The Lib Dems should join up with Labour splitters, should the split take place.
The 2017 general election was supposed to be the one in which the so-called Lib Dem fightback made itself clearly seen. We all know how that turned out. You could lay a lot of the blame on Tim Farron's leadership and the whole 'homosexuality is a sin' debacle, but this would be unfair. The party has struggled for definition since Iraq ceased to be such an issue ten or so years back. The party lost five seats in 2010 after the Cleggmania poll bounce, which suggests that had the bump from the debates not occurred, the party could have done much worse in that general election. Whatever the reason, an election which was supposed to represent a revival of the Liberal Democrats saw the party treading water.

Should there be a new centrist party in town, the Lib Dems should hitch their wagon to it. Perhaps an alliance like in the '80s, who knows. But it certainly shouldn't fight against such a centrist force, were it to become a reality.

4. Needed: a leader who is so charismatic and inspiring that no amount of crap slung at her or him would be enough to stop her or his unstoppable rise to No. 10.

This is so key – and yet as I've spent a lot of this portion of the book saying, there is no one who jumps out at me who fits this description. The thing is, often these figures seemingly come from nowhere. Who knows, perhaps David Miliband really will return, find some way into Parliament and turn out to be as good as everyone in the centre of British politics hopes he would be. More likely, the person who fills this role will be someone neither you nor I have heard of or at least thought of at the time of writing.

5. It has to be about so much more than Europe.

What unites a lot of Labour moderates, Lib Dems and centrists in general is a melancholy surrounding Brexit. While Brexit may provide some legroom for the Tories to screw up and for the hoped-for Bregret to kick in, for centrists to rely on this happening would be foolish. Thinking of some way for Britain to either remain in the European Union or one day rejoin it needs to be put to one side, as the public is simply too far from this position as it stands. As far as Europe goes, providing an effective opposition to May and her party during the Brexit proceedings is all this bunch can do. That would be no small feat in itself, particularly given how poorly it has been done thus far by Corbyn and co. Either the country begins to change its mind on Brexit as a result of it going extremely poorly, or it does not. Pro-Europeans' hope that the country would 'come to its senses' has proven unfounded. While the 'enemies of the people' motif has thankfully calmed down, it is clear that challenging the wisdom of the masses hasn't panned out, as it never does in democracy. To paraphrase a much better man on this subject, when people ask for something in a democracy, you have to give it to them until they are sick of it, not tell them they were wrong to have asked for it in the first place.

The Labour moderates need to realise they have run out of space, time and excuses. It is Corbyn's party now, and it is difficult to see what could change that. Perhaps a crushing general election defeat, but I'm not sure even that would do it. Corbyn is a rock star now to a generation of Labour activists. I think actual results are immaterial from here on in, particularly as many of them proclaim Corbyn 'the real Prime Minister' already. Every member of the PLP must now ask themselves: do

I really want Jeremy Corbyn to be Prime Minister? The answer to that one should guide their decision on what to do next.

Meanwhile, the Tories are not without plenty of problems of their own. They have a very sticky Brexit negotiation to navigate in the coming parliament, one that could present all sorts of difficulties for them, both internally and externally. A split within the parliamentary party as to whether or not to take a deal, whether to walk away entirely or get locked into a transitional deal that could last for decades, if not for ever – on the other side, the public is dissatisfied with what we end up with, post-negotiations. And all to be done without a parliamentary majority and with a Prime Minister whose authority has been fatally undermined. Furthermore, the 2017 general election demonstrated how vulnerable the Tory vote is.

The relative unity within the Labour Party after the unexpected election result could be very short-lived (in fact, I'm scared of it even being intact by the time this goes to print). MPs who thought they were gone for sure are back in the Commons, and are willing to forgive Corbyn a lot as a result. But that can't and won't last for ever, particularly as Corbyn missed the chance to unite the PLP and seems determined to continue his war against the Labour moderates. If the Tories can dig in,

Labour could destroy themselves via internecine warfare on Brexit once again, this time to much worse effect.

Meanwhile, a centrist party that could navigate the chaos seems a distant hope, one seemingly destined to remain unfulfilled. But who knows: perhaps the need for such a party will become so great, the times will simply will it into being.